Sidney Joseph Madge

Moulton Church and its Bells

With a complete Summary of the Bells in the several Parishes of

Northamptonshire

Sidney Joseph Madge

Moulton Church and its Bells
With a complete Summary of the Bells in the several Parishes of Northamptonshire

ISBN/EAN: 9783337161743

Printed in Europe, USA, Canada, Australia, Japan

Cover: Foto ©ninafisch / pixelio.de

More available books at **www.hansebooks.com**

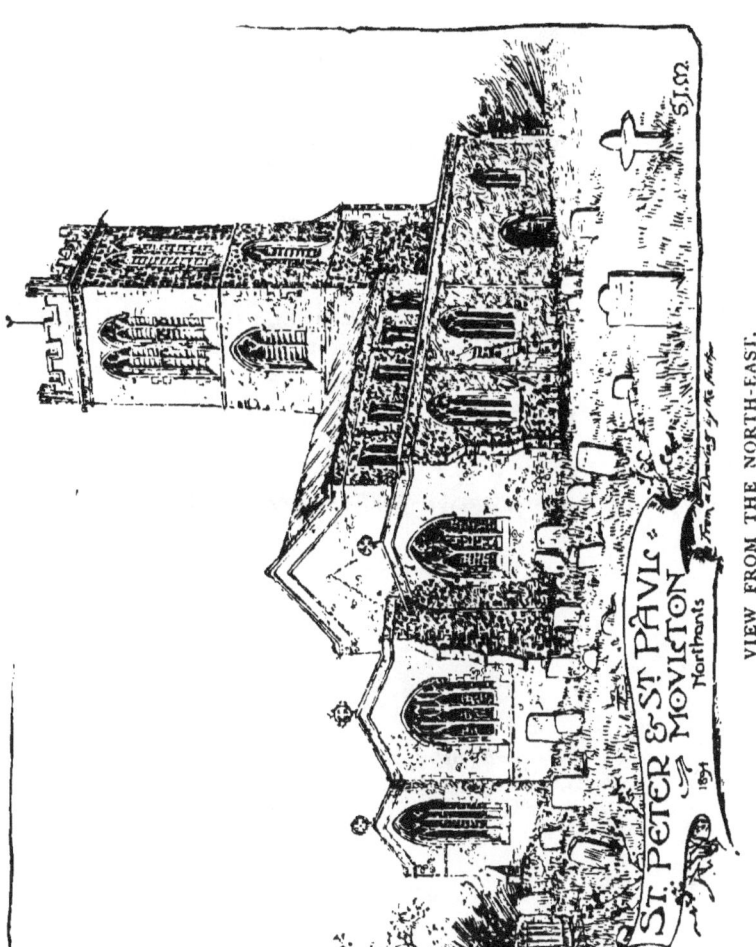

VIEW FROM THE NORTH-EAST.

MOULTON CHURCH

AND ITS BELLS.

WITH

A COMPLETE SUMMARY OF THE BELLS IN THE SEVERAL
PARISHES OF NORTHAMPTONSHIRE;

ALSO,

A Comprehensive Bibliography on 'Bells.'

BY

SIDNEY MADGE,

Member of the Northampton and Oakham Architectural Society;
Editorial Correspondent of 'Gloucestershire Notes and Queries;'
Author of 'A History of Moulton Parish Church,' etc.

WITH ORIGINAL ILLUSTRATIONS BY THE AUTHOR.

LONDON:
ELLIOT STOCK, 62, PATERNOSTER ROW, E.C.
1895.

To

MY BROTHER,

ERNEST B. WILMER MADGE,

ORGANIST OF THE PARISH CHURCH OF ST. ALDATE'S, OXFORD,

THIS VOLUME IS,

WITH WARMEST AFFECTION,

Dedicated.

LIST OF ILLUSTRATIONS.

	PAGE
MOULTON CHURCH FROM THE N.E.	*Frontispiece*
MOULTON CHURCH IN THE FOURTEENTH CENTURY	21
THE TOWER, SKETCHED FROM THE S.W.	25
THE CHURCH, BEFORE THE CIVIL WAR	27
RINGING CHAMBER, AS RESTORED 1884	33
ARNOLD'S ORNAMENTAL DESIGN, TENOR BELL	38
INTERIOR OF THE UPPER BELFRY	44
HEAD OF KING HENRY III., 1216-1272	45
THE ORIGINAL BELFRY, INTERIOR VIEW	47
AMONG THE BELLS	53
CONSECRATION CROSSES AND FLORAL ORNAMENT	59

PREFACE.

THIS volume, written to commemorate the centenary of Moulton Bells, is arranged on the following plan :

Part I. deals with the history from earliest times of 'Moulton Church and its Bells;' and an appendix is added which contains much interesting information concerning the parish and its associations.

Part II. records the church bells of Northamptonshire parishes as known to exist in 1552, 1700, and at the present time. Extracts also are given from the inventories of the Tudor period.

Part III. forms a 'Comprehensive Bibliography on Bells,' and includes : (1) The 'Subject-Catalogue' (with press marks) of the Bodleian Library; (2) Foreign Works, 1416, *et seq.*; (3) English Writers since 1668; (4) a Collection of Pamphlets and Miscellaneous Works; and (5) References to Periodical Literature, wherein matters about bells have been treated since 1730. These references are indexed under the heads 'Signed Articles,' 'General Matters,' 'Special Matters,' and 'Topographical.'

The second section of this work is based on the volume of 'Northamptonshire Church Bells,' published in 1878, by the late Thomas North, F.S.A. ; whilst the works of the late Rev. T. Ellacombe, F.S.A., have been freely consulted in preparing the Bibliography in Part III.

I wish to tender my grateful acknowledgments to many kind friends for their valuable assistance and advice. In correcting and revising the proof-sheets, the aid of Mr. Christopher A. Markham, F.S.A., has been most generous and untiring. My thanks also are due to the Rev. Charles D. P. Davies, M.A., of East Marden Rectory, Chichester, editor of the 'Campanological Section' of *Church Bells*, for kindly revising a considerable portion of the manuscript, and rendering other valuable assistance; to the Rev. Alexander Mackintosh, M.A., of Coleford, Sandown, Isle of Wight (Vicar of Moulton from 1888 to 1892), for much practical help and encouragement; the Rev. R. C. Faithfull, M.A., Curate-in-charge 1886 to 1888; Mr. John Taylor, editor of *Northamptonshire Notes and Queries ;* Mr. T. J. George, F.G.S., Librarian of the Northampton Free Library; the staff of the Bodleian Library; and the bell-ringers of Moulton Church.

I would take this opportunity of expressing my many and great obligations for the courtesy shown me by Sir John Stainer, and the personal assistance freely rendered by E. W. Byron Nicholson, Esq., M.A., Librarian of the Bodleian Library, Oxford.

SIDNEY MADGE.

CHELTENHAM,
  June 4, 1895.

CONTENTS.

PART I.

CHAPTER I.

MOULTON, VILLAGE AND PARISH.

                                                            PAGE

Situation — Derivation — Forests — The Coritani — Druids — Roman Roads—Saxon Manor—Norman Castle—Waltheof, 1065 to 1076—Countess Judith—Lords of the Manor—Domesday Accounts—Population, 1701 to 1891—*Moulton Park:* its Associations, References in 1086, 1201, and 1531—*Thorpelands:* Assassination of Sir William Tresham, 1451; acquired by Sir William Wilmer, 1644—*Moulton Grange:* Pytchley Hunt—Late Mr. and Mrs. Nethercote—*Moulton Grounds:* Castle of the Fitz-Johns—*Moulton Chapels:* Carey's House—Baptist Chapel—Memorial Tablet—Succession of Baptist Ministers -   -   -   -   -   13

CHAPTER II.

MOULTON CHURCH AND ITS ASSOCIATIONS.

Seventh Century edifice—Saxon Church destroyed, Tenth Century—Similar Fate, 1017—St. Andrew's Priory, 1084—Grimbald's Gift confirmed—Vicarage endowed, 1209—Rectory, 1254—Taxation of Pope Nicholas, 1291—Bishop of Lincoln's Mandate, 1298—Possessions of St. Andrew's Priory in Moulton, 1084, 1133, 1200, 1291, 1535; Fineshade Priory, 1291, 1535, 1545; Ouston Abbey, 1291; St. Frideswide's, Oxford, 1291; St. Alban's Abbey, 1291—Later Events, 1298 to 1500—The Vicarage, 1535—Dissolution of St. Andrew's, 1538—Vicars, 1540 to 1688—Curious Presentment, 1578—The Puritans—Church Restorations—Visit of the late Archbishop Magee -   19

CHAPTER III.

THE TOWER AND ITS CONTENTS: PRE-REFORMATION HISTORY.

Bells, 680 A.D.—Substitutes in Early Church—Erection of Tower—Upper Belfry, Fifteenth Century—Decorated Bell-chamber—Spire added—New Bells, 1450 to 1540—Traditions—St. Andrew's Monastery Bells—Inventory of Priory, 1538   ·   24

CHAPTER IV.

FROM EDWARD VI. TO WILLIAM III.

King's Commissions—Inventory of Moulton Church Goods, 1552—A Famous 'Mote Bell'—Resignation of Vicars—Reign of the Puritans—Destruction of Pinnacles and Spire—Cromwell and his Army, 15,000 Men, at Northampton—Loss of the 'Sanctus Bell'—New Bells, 1664—Later History, 1700—Inscription on an Ancient Bell at Moulton, *c.* 1230—Particulars of the Early Bells—Church Plate · · 28

CHAPTER V.

THE YEAR 1795.

Churchwardens' Accounts—Loyal Peals, Birthday of King George III.—Letters between Rev. W. Stanton and Mr. Edward Arnold—Last Occasion of ringing the Old Peal—The Curfew's Last Dirge · · · · · 31

CHAPTER VI.

ON THE ROAD : THE JOURNEY HOME.

Through Northamptonshire—Market Harborough reached—Leicestershire Route — At the Foundry — Contemporary Records—The Thirteenth-Century Tenor Bell, Inscription and Size—Analytical Tables of Route—The Welcome Home—Baptismal Ceremony—Particulars of the New Peal · 35

CHAPTER VII.

THE NEW PEAL, AND ITS SUBSEQUENT HISTORY.

Inscriptions on Treble and Tenor—Other Churches with same Mottoes—The Rev. William Stanton, M.A., 1738 to 1768—Memorial Tablet to the Stanton Family—Alterations and Restorations, 1816, 1818, 1847, 1848, 1849, 1853, 1855, 1878, 1880, 1883, 1884 to 1886—Vestry Regulations—The Church Clock and its Caretakers—The Chimers—Restoration of Tower and Bells, 1884—Discovery of Arnold's Bill - · 39

CHAPTER VIII.

LEGENDS THAT LINGER.

St. Andrew's Monastery Bells—Ruins of St. John Baptist Church, Boughton — Broughton Church mistaken — Cromwell's Mighty Deeds—Robbery in a Belfry—The Tenor Bell once more—Popes on the Scene, 1216 to 1272—Inventory of Bells at Boughton Parish Church—A 'Malden' Bell at Moulton—Weston Favell Bells mistaken—Overstone and Sywell Bells · 45

CHAPTER IX.

PECULIAR USES AND CUSTOMS.

Chiming—Melodies—The 'Ave Maria'—General Uses - - 48
Part I. *Daily Bells:* Regulation, 1848—(1) Harvest—(2) Spring and Summer—(3) Autumn and Winter—(4) Noonday—(5) Curfew - - - - - - - 49
Part II. *Sunday Bells:* (6) Early Morning—(7) Second Hour—(8) Matins—(9) Conclusion of Service—(10) Sermon Bell, ii.—(11) Afternoon Service—(12) Sermon Bell, iii.—(13) Evensong - - - - - - - 50
Part III. *Death Bells:* (14) Winding Bell—(15) Death Knell—(16) Infant's Passing Bell—(17) Funerals—(18) Dumb Peals - - - - - - - - 51
Part IV. *Miscellaneous Customs:* (19) Church Festivals—(20) Loyal Peals—(21) New Year's Eve—(22) Vestry Bell—(23) Induction—(24) Gleaning—(25) Plough Monday—(26) Execution of Charles I.—(27) St. George's Day—(28) St. Andrew's Day—(29) St. Paul's Day—(30) St. Stephen's Day—(31) Soulmas—(32) Lady Day—(33) Mote Bell—(34) Dole Meadow—(35) Apprentice—(36) Seed-sowing—(37) Harvest—(38) Sacrament Bell—(39) Sacring Bell - - - - - - - - 52

APPENDIX TO PART I.

I. VICARS OF MOULTON SINCE 1200 A.D. - - - 54
II. TABLE SHOWING THE NUMBER OF VICARS INSTITUTED IN EACH CENTURY - - - - 55
III. PRIORS OF ST. ANDREW'S MONASTERY, NORTHAMPTON 55
IV. CARTA AD SANCTI ANDREÆ NORTHAMPTONÆ PRIORATUM SPECTANTES:
    i. Carta Simonis primi Comitis - - - 56
    ii. Carta Simonis comitis, primi fundatoris - - 56
    iii. Confirmatio Donationum, per Hugonem Lincolniensem episcopam - - - - 57
    iv. Carta Regis Henrici primi donatorum concessiones ratificans - - - - - - 57
    v. Valor Ecclesiasticus temp. Henry VIII. - - 57
    vi. 'Book of Demaynes' in 1538 - - - 58
    vii. Caput' Ministrorum Domini Regis temp. Hen. VIII. 58
    viii. Miscellanea: (*a*) Abstract of Priory Register: (*b*) 'Computus' of 34 Hen. VI.; (*c*) State of the Priory in 1538 - - - - 58
V. INVENTORY OF MOULTON CHURCH, 1552 - - 59
VI. INSCRIPTIONS ON THE BELLS, 1795 - - - 59
VII. TABLE OF WEIGHTS AND DIAMETERS, ETC., OF BOTH PEALS - - - - - - - 60
VIII. TABLE OF THE DISTINCTIVE USES OF EACH BELL - 60

Contents

	PAGE
IX. TABLE OF EXPENDITURE ON MOULTON BELLS SINCE 1778	61
X. EXTRACTS FROM CHURCHWARDENS' ACCOUNTS:	
i. Cost of the Present Peal	61
ii. Concerning the Clock	62
iii. Bell-Ringing and Ringers	64
iv. Bell-ropes	64
v. Miscellaneous Items	65

PART II.

A SUMMARY OF NORTHAMPTONSHIRE BELLS, WITH EXTRACTS FROM INVENTORIES, ETC.	66

PART III.

	PAGE
BIBLIOTHECA CAMPANALOGICA:	
Sec. I. Foreign Works, 1416 *et seq.*	78
„ II. English Works, 1668-1895	84
„ III. Miscellanea, 1495 *et seq.*; comprising Tracts, MSS., and special portions of various works, English and Foreign	90
PERIODICAL LITERATURE:	
Sec. IV. Signed Articles, etc.	94
„ V. General Matters about Bells	95
„ VI. Special Matters about Bells	96
„ VII. Topographical References	97

PART I.

CHAPTER I.

MOULTON, VILLAGE AND PARISH.

Situation — Derivation — Forests — The Coritani — Druids — Roman Roads — Saxon Manor — Norman Castle — Waltheof, 1065 to 1076 — —Countess Judith — Lords of the Manor — Domesday Accounts — Population, 1701 to 1891 — Moulton Park : Its Associations, References in 1086, 1201, 1531 ; population, 1841-1891 — Thorpelands : Assassination of Sir William Tresham, 1451 ; acquired by Sir William Wilmer, 1644 — Moulton Grange : Pytchley Hunt — Late Mr. and Mrs. Nethercote — Moulton Grounds : Castle of the Fitz-Johns — Moulton Chapels : Carey's House — Baptist Chapel — Memorial Tablet — Succession of Baptist Ministers.

A DREAMY old township is Moulton, full of 'old-world memories.' It is situated within four miles of Northampton, midway between the main road to Market Harborough and the North, and the main road to Kettering and Stamford. Much uncertainty exists as to the derivation of the name. Baker, the historian, thinks Moulton may have received its name from the British *Mul*, a stream, or perhaps from *Mola*, a mill; but others hold that it was the *Mele-ton*, or 'embanked and protected enclosure' of British chiefs, long before the arrival of the Roman legions.

Before the birth of Christ large forests covered the land. As time passed these were partially cleared and rendered fit for human habitation. In the great central forest, which extended over the whole of Northamptonshire, savage tribes made their conquests, until overcome and exterminated by more powerful foes. The Coritani were among the first to acquire undisputed possession of the land in the east of this forest, and, becoming superior in arms and in numbers, pushed their way westward for a considerable distance; in this manner was the district around Moulton acquired.

From Brixworth the Romans made a road through Moulton and thence to Holcot.* At Moulton this 'Way' passed through the ancient 'Grove,'† where Druids had previously set up their temple and sacrificed to their gods. But civilization threw down the rude altars and erected a Christian church near the spot.

The manor in Saxon times was of large extent, with vast ponds surrounding the manor-house; here, at the time of the Norman Conquest, Ailricus the Thegn resided. William I., however, dispossessed him, and gave his inheritance to the Countess Judith, his own half-sister. Waltheof, son of Siward the Dane, Earl of Northumbria, after resisting the Conqueror for a long time, was captured in January, 1070, near the mouth of the Tees. On submitting to the King's mercy, not only was he pardoned and reinstated in his earldoms of Northamptonshire and Huntingdon, but the hand of the Countess Judith was given him in marriage. Alas! Judith proved false, betrayed her husband, and he was executed at Winchester, May 31, 1076.

Moulton is thus recorded in Domesday Book:

| (i.) IN MALESLEA HUND.— Rex tenet *Torp*. . . . Huic Manerio pertinet *Multone*. Ibi est i. hida. et dimidia. et i. bovata terræ. | (i.) IN MALESLEA HUNDRED. —The King holds Kingsthorp. . . . To this manor pertains *Multone*. There is 1 hide and a half and 1 bovate of land. |

---

* Mr. C. A. Markham's opinion on this point is interesting. 'My idea,' he says, 'is that their road was from the high road by Boughton House, then to Old Boughton Church and straight into Moulton. This would make a direct road, with one bend, leading straight to Moulton Church.'

† Completely destroyed by a gale, Sunday, March 24, 1895.

(ii.) IN SPEREHOU HD.—Idem Willelmus tenet de Roberto ii. hidas et unam virgatam terræ et dimidiam, in *Moltone*. Terra est v. carucarum. In dominio sunt iii. carucæ cum i. servo. et vii. villani et iiii. bordarii habent ii. carucas. Ibi molinus de viii. denariis. Valuit xx. solidos. Modo l. solidos. Thori tenuit.

(iii.) IN WIMARESLEA HUNDREDO ET DIMIDIO.—Idem tenet de Comitissa iii hidas et unam virgatam terræ in *Multone*. Terra est vi. carucarum et dimidæ. In dominio est una. et xii. villani cum iiii. bordariis habent v. carucas. et dimidiam. Valuit et valet xl. solidos. Ailricus libere tenuit tempore Regis Edwardo.

(ii.) IN SPELHO HUND.—The same William holds of Robert [de Buci] 2 hides and 1 virgate and a half of land in *Moltone*. There is land for 5 ploughs. In demesne there are 3 ploughs, with 1 serf; and 7 villeins and 4 bordars have 2 ploughs. There is a mill rendering 8 pence. It is worth 20s., now [it is worth] 50s. Thori held [it].

(iii.) IN WIMARESLEA HUND. & HALF.—The same [Grimbald] holds of the Countess [Judith] 3 hides and 1 virgate of land in *Multone*. There is land for 6 ploughs and a half. In demesne there is 1 plough; and 12 villeins, with 4 bordars, have 5 ploughs and a half. It was and is worth 40s. Ailric held [it] freely in King Edward's time.

Moulton parish, which consists of some 3,000 acres in the Hundred of Spelhoe, is situated at an elevation of from 300 to 450 feet above Liverpool mean water-mark; consequently, the place attracted many visitors and invalids in times past on account of its healthy and pleasant situation. Its 'chalybeate waters,' moreover, had for several centuries been procured by patients, and large quantities are said to have been sent to various parts of the kingdom annually. The population of the village in recent years has decreased, mainly owing to agricultural depression. The figures, since the sixteenth century, are as follows:

Years.	Population.	Years.	Population.	Years.	Population.	Years.	Population.
1701	450	1811	928	1841	1,368	1871	1,692
1791	670*	1821	1,200*	1851	1,524	1881	1,483
1801	843	1831	1,334	1861	1,848	1891	1,382

* Estimated.

MOULTON PARK, comprising about 450 acres, now forms a separate parish. It was formerly extra-parochial, and for centuries existed as a feudal appendage to Northampton Castle. Occasionally it was referred to as 'the King's Park at Northampton,' as, for instance, in this extract from the Chancellor's Roll, 3rd John (1201) : ' In the purchase of hay for feeding the beasts in the Park at Northampton, thirty-seven shillings.' In Domesday Book *Moulton Park* is twice recorded:

(i.) IN STOTFALD HUND.—Biscop tenet de Comitissa dimidiam hidam in *Muletone*. Terra est i. carucæ. Ipsa ibi est cum ii. villanis et ii. bordariis. Valet x. solidos.

(i.) Biscop holds of the Countess half a hide in *Moulton Park*. There is land for 1 plough. That is there with 2 villeins and 2 bordars. It is worth 10s.

(ii.) IN MALESLEA HUND.—Idem tenet unam virgatam terræ in *Muletone*. Ibi i. sochmannus habet dimidiam carucam. et reddit xxxiii. denarios.

(ii.) The same [Hugh] holds one virgate of land in *Moulton Park*. There 1 sochman has half a plough, and renders 33 pence.

Certain villages were responsible for the murage of the park. Culworth accounts, for instance, have this entry in 1531 : 'Item paid to Moulton Park 4d.' Henry VIII. in the same year commanded ' the officers of our forest of Sawcey, and of our park at Moulton ' to deliver ' such and as many oaks, convertable for posts and rayles, with the lops, tops, and bark of the same, sufficient for enlarging the park at Hartwell, and making a new lodge there.'

Moulton Park had a population in 1841 of 18 ; in 1861, 8 ; 1871, 11 ; 1881, 45 ; and at the last census, 42.

THORPELANDS is an ancient enclosure of about 200 acres, in Moulton parish. It came into possession of the Wilmers, baronets, prior to 1644. The place is memorable for the assassination of Sir William Tresham in 1451.[*] Sir William was returning home to Sywell, when, on stop-

* *Northampton N. and Q.*, iii., p. 4.

ping to say his Matins, one Symon Norwich suddenly surprised him, and cruelly thrust him through with a spear. ' His servants coming up presently, found him in this deplorable state, and for the better carrying of him back to Northampton, they cut off each end of the spear that stuck out at his back and front; but when they reached the town, and pulled out the rest of the truncheon, the patient died.'

MOULTON GRANGE, in the north-west, is one of the best-known houses in the ' Pytchley Country.' Here the author of ' The Pytchley Hunt, Past and Present,' lived, and here, too, he, the late Henry Osmond Nethercote, died, 1886. Mrs. Nethercote, amid much sorrow, was laid to rest in the churchyard in May, 1890. The deeds of both will be long cherished.

MOULTON GROUNDS, just outside the village, along the Pitsford road, is most prettily situated, and occupies the site where once stood a castle of the Fitz-Johns. In Norman times all three—castle, church, and manor-house —were within bowshot, thus affording excellent protection to the inhabitants.

Besides the ancient church, there are in the village chapels for Wesleyans, Baptists, and Primitive Methodists. The Baptist chapel has peculiar interest, for it is believed to have been one of the earliest founded in Northamptonshire, on a site, tradition says, which was given by one of Cromwell's troopers. In a house near the chapel the renowned William Carey lived, making shoes and keeping school the while. This remarkable man was born at Paulerspery, near Towcester, August 17, 1761, and in 1786 was appointed pastor of the little village chapel at Moulton. In 1793 he founded the Missionary Society. Carey was a great botanist, and his botanical gardens at Serampore are said to have contained 3,000 species of plants. A memorial tablet on the north wall of the chapel at Moulton bears this inscription:

'This Tablet was erected in memory of the Illustrious WM. CAREY, D.D., who was the honoured founder of this place of worship, and who for four years was the devoted pastor of this church—He afterwards became the evangelist of India, Professor of Sanscrit in the College of Fort William, and the Father of Modern Missions—He died at Serampore, June 9th, 1834. Aged 72 years.'

The story of William Carey is well told by Marianne Farningham in a poem, 'The Shoemaker Missionary,' in which she says :

> 'So he took
> The little village church they offered him,
> And when the stipend, ten or fifteen pounds,
> Proved all too meagre, made the village shoes,
> And mended them ; and taught the village boys,
> Making a globe of leather for his school,
> And giving lessons in geography—
> Chiefly of India. . . .
> But the Moulton fields
> Were his prayer-places, and the silent trees
> Looked down the while he made his high resolves ;
> And the calm stars smiled with approving light,
> And now and then the wakeful nightingale
> Might hear another plaintive lay than hers
> Break through the stillness, and, "O Lord, how long?"
> Come from the lips of Carey.'

Succession of Baptist Ministers at Moulton :

i. GENERAL BAPTISTS.
c. 1715. William Stanger.
   1742-) Thomas Stanger and
   1768.) William Painter.

ii. PARTICULAR, or CALVINISTIC.
c. 1750. George Evans.
   [No further record.]

iii. PRESENT SUCCESSION.
1785. William Carey.

1789-1795. Edward Sharman.
1802. Thomas Burridge.
1818. Francis Wheeler.
1854. Joseph Lea.
1867. John R. Parker.
1879. George Phillips.
1882. W. A. Wicks.
1888. L. E. Bartlett.
1891. Frederick Watts.

CHAPTER II.

MOULTON CHURCH AND ITS ASSOCIATIONS.

Seventh Century Edifice—Saxon Church destroyed, Tenth Century—Similar Fate, 1017—St. Andrew's Priory, 1084—Grimbald's Gift confirmed—Vicarage endowed, 1209—Rectory, 1254—Taxation of Pope Nicholas, 1291—Bishop of Lincoln's Mandate, 1298—Possessions of St. Andrew's Priory in Moulton, 1084, 1133, 1200, 1291, 1535; Fineshade Priory, 1291, 1535, 1545; Ouston Abbey, 1291; St. Frideswide's, Oxford, 1291; St. Alban's Abbey, 1291—Later Events, 1298 to 1500—The Vicarage. 1535—Dissolution of St. Andrew's, 1538—Vicars, 1540 to 1688—The Puritans—Church Restorations—Visit of the late Archbishop Magee.

EARLY in the seventh century, a little wooden church, dedicated to St. Peter, was erected at Moulton. The situation, in many ways pleasant, was doubtless chosen for the purpose of defence. It was perched on the summit of a hill 340 feet above the sea, at the foot of which two streams met. On the west the hill descended abruptly, and below this were clustered the rude huts of the people. A mere track constituted the street, giving access to the tower in times of danger. Arrows would then fly fast from the narrow loopholes, while the thane in his moated castle would hasten to defend himself from all attacks.

The Saxon church was eventually fired by the Danes, who, in the tenth century, devastated the locality with fire and sword. Another rose upon its ashes, only to meet a similar fate, under similar circumstances, in 1017. Shortly afterwards a third building was begun, a considerable portion of which still exists.

In the year 1084, Grimbald the Norman gave to St. Andrew's Priory, Northampton, 'the chutch and tythes of "Multon"'; subsequently, 'Robert Grimbald confirmed his father's grant of the church and seven virgates of land " in the same township," which were further confirmed by his successors,' and afterwards by William Mandeville, Earl of Essex, who died in 1220. The priory had other possessions in Moulton. Alexander de Multon made a grant of a virgate of land; and about 1133 King Henry I. presented 'two virgates and the tythes of a mill called "Canchesmilne."' At the close of the thirteenth century—it was during the vicariate of Robert de Botelbrigge, 1287-1313—a mandate was issued by Oliver Sutton, Bishop of Lincoln (in whose diocese Moulton then lay), commanding the inhabitants of Moulton to rebuild 'the Church, Tower, and Churchyard,' which were 'miserably in ruins'—the cause of this being the 'Barons' War,' thirty years before.

The Vicarage was endowed in 1209, under the direction of Bishop Wells. Nearly half a century later, 1254, it is recorded that the 'Rectory of Moulton' was 'rated at 12 marks with a pension of xiijs. ivd. out of the Vicarage, which was not then valued.' Passing forward to the 20th Edward I., when Pope Nicholas (1288-1292) ordered a new taxation of ecclesiastical property, we find that five monasteries were at this time interested in the parish:

'i. *St. Andrew's Priory lands*. In 1291 the temporal possessions of the priory here were rated at £2 1s. 4d. per annum in rents, and 4s. in land; and "in the ecclesiastical survey of 1535 (26 Hen. VIII.), at £2 14s. 6d. per annum, demised to Thomas Chipsey for a term of years."

'ii. *Fineshade Priory* had lands in "Multon" valued at £2 2s. per annum in 1291, and at £1 per annum in the ecclesiastical survey of 1535. "In 35 Hen. VIII. (1545), these lands and tenements were granted to John Bellew and Edward Bailes in fee, at 2s. rent per annum."

'iii. *Ouston Abbey* also had rents in "Multon," which, in the taxation of Pope Nicholas were valued at 5s. per annum.

MOULTON CHURCH IN THE FOURTEENTH CENTURY.

'iv. *St. Frideswide's Priory, Oxford*, had "5 virgates of land, granted and confirmed by King John, which were rated at 12s. rent per annum in the taxation of Pope Nicholas."

'v. *St. Alban's Abbey* had 3s. rent per annum in 1291.'*

Bishop Sutton's mandate of 1298 was obeyed by Vicar Robert de Botelbrigge, who caused the tower and church to be rebuilt, adding at the same time a beautiful aisle on the south side. This was dedicated to St. Paul. Late in

* 'History of Moulton Parish Church,' by the Author.

the fourteenth century, a south porch was added, the clerestory built, and the roofs lowered successively throughout. During the next century the present elegant bell-chamber was erected. It is, however, a matter of uncertainty as to the exact date when the spire was added.

Three years before the dissolution of St. Andrew's Monastery, in 1535 to be exact, a record shows that Moulton Vicarage was 'rated at xv^l, out of which was deducted iij^s for synodals and procurations, and xiij^s iv^d for a yearly pension to the Prior and Convent of St. Andrew;' also at this time the 'Rectory' was let out by lease from the convent to 'Edward Watson and his assigns for xvj^l a year.' When Henry VIII.'s displeasure fell upon the monastery, in the year of grace 1538, the Prior was presented to the living of Moulton, 'as a reward for his submissive acquiescence to the King's Commissioners.' His institution took place on July 31, 1540, amid public rejoicings; but his residence here was of short duration. Peterborough was raised to the dignity of a see in 1541, and Abree became its Dean.—A curious presentment was made to Bishop Scambler in 1578, stating that 'Joane Tymms is a scolde, & soweth discorde among neighbors!'

Among subsequent vicars was one, Fleshware by name, twice presented to the living—on the first occasion by 'John Freeman, of Great Billing, Esq.,' on January 14, 1607, and on the next by 'John Smith, of Marston St. Lawrence, Gent., by a grant from Sir Francis Freeman, of Lothbury Bucks, and instituted 11th June same year.' He enjoyed the unenviable distinction of being Vicar for almost a quarter of a century, during the whole of which time he resided elsewhere! Later, February 22, 1639-40, the famous divine, Edward Bagshaw, was inducted; but very shortly afterwards the Commissioners assembled at Northampton summarily ejected him, and put into his office two intruders. Bagshaw, however, outlived both, and in 1660 was restored by Charles II. He died at the time of the Revolution of 1688, half a century after his preferment.

It is needless to dwell upon the events which followed, for they tell of little else than oft-repeated restorations. Exactly 800 years after the time of Grimbald the Norman the Moulton Church Restoration Committee met at the Vicarage to consider seriously what steps should be taken to preserve the edifice from utter ruin. The result of that meeting was entered by the late Henry Osmond Nethercote in the minute-book, which states that on November 3, 1884, the committee resolved 'that the roofs of the nave and two aisles, and the parapets of the tower, be thoroughly restored, and the northern arcade made safe; also, if funds will permit, to open out and repair the western arch; all at a sum not exceeding £1,200.' Yet, before the restoration was effected the sum expended reached, not £1,200, but £3,500; and on that glorious June 15, 1886, when the late Archbishop Magee re-opened the church, in the presence of a large concourse of people (among whom were nearly a hundred clergy), white-robed choristers, for the first time since the Reformation, led the long procession, singing:

> 'Lift the strain of high thanksgiving!
> Tread with songs the hallowed way!
> Praise our fathers' God for mercies
> New to us their sons to-day:
> Here they built for Him a dwelling,
> Served him here in ages past,
> Fix'd it for His sure possession,
> Holy ground, while time shall last.'

The organist on this memorable occasion was one whom a brother may be pardoned in mentioning—Mr. E. B. Wilmer Madge, the present organist of St. Aldate's, Oxford.

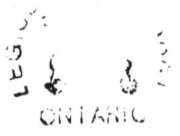

CHAPTER III.

THE TOWER AND ITS CONTENTS: PRE-REFORMATION HISTORY.

Bells, 680 A.D.—Substitutes in Early Church—Erection of Tower—Upper Belfry, Fifteenth Century—Decorated Bell-chamber—Spire added—New Bells, 1450 to 1540—Traditions—St. Andrew's Monastery Bells—Inventory of Priory, 1538.

AT what period a bell was first introduced into the church at Moulton must for ever remain a matter of uncertainty. Bells were practically unknown in England before 680 A.D., and even then their use was restricted to the larger monasteries. The early church, therefore, it may safely be concluded, had not in its possession a bell of any kind. It was usual at that period to call the Christians to prayer in two ways—by 'runners,' and by striking together pieces of 'sacred boards.' For perhaps three centuries the latter method was in vogue. The second building doubtless had a small bell in its turret at some early period, in addition to the usual 'lytel hande bell.' During the eleventh century there was at least one bell, and there is every reason to believe that another—probably the gift of the manorial lord—was added shortly afterwards. In the thirteenth century the present tower was commenced and contained, in all probability, the first *ring of bells* on completion.

The tower has considerable elegance. It is lofty and

noble in appearance, and, as is the case with Decorated towers, is placed at the west end of the church.* The battlemented parapet has at the angles the remains of what originally were four beautiful pinnacles—now irretrievably lost. The face of the tower is divided into four stages; but at present the old and new belfries are open to the roof, and so form a single chamber, about 40 feet in

THE TOWER FROM THE SOUTH-WEST.

height—one of the finest in Northamptonshire. The four stages consist of a 'ringing chamber' (*circa* 1250), 30 feet high; a 'clock chamber'; the 'original belfry chamber,' in the Decorated style; and the 'new belfry chamber' (Perpendicular), erected about 1422.

* See Parker's 'A B C of Gothic Architecture,' in which this tower is regarded as a typical one.

The tower was completed at an uncertain date. The work, however, progressed under Thomas de Ryhall (1263-1280), Ralph de Stangoot (1280-1287), and Robert de Botelbrigge (1287-1313)—priests and vicars of Moulton. Upon its completion several new bells, doubtless, made their appearance: the original belfry still contains evidence as to their existence, as also to the position of the framework supporting them. Two of the Decorated windows (those on the west and east) were partially built up, and remain so to this day. Clearly, the bells were hung at a height less than 40 feet above the surface of the ground.

In the early years of the fifteenth century, the elegant upper belfry was erected, the style being Perpendicular, of a more praiseworthy type than that attempted in the windows of the south aisle. Into this beautiful chamber were the bells removed from their former position in the Decorated belfry; and about the same time a spire was added, making the total height about 110 feet.* The ringing chamber was immediately beneath the clock-room; but in 1884 it was removed, the tower again thrown open, and ringing from the ground substituted.

Between 1450 and 1540 two new bells were added to the four already existing in the tower, thus making a total ring of six. It is, however, a disputed point whence they came, or at what date they were hung within the new belfry. A tradition is recorded that they were received from St. Andrew's Monastery, but this is highly improbable. At the time of its dissolution the priory possessed nine bells, which were sold to the merchants of Northampton for the sum of £100. The following extracts from the inventory of 1538 are interesting:

---

* Writing on January 9, 1895, on behalf of the Director-General of the Ordnance Survey, Lieutenant-Colonel Johnston, R.E., informed the Author that the present height of the tower above the surface of the ground is 79 feet 3 inches, i.e., 420 feet above the sea.

'Monasterium sive nuper Prioratus Sa. Andree infra Villam North. in com. North., 1538 :

'Belles, ix.— { Solde by the sayd Commissioners in great to the merchaunts of the towne, for the some of ... ... } c*l*.

* * * * *

'Wagies and rewardes. { To xiij religious parsons xx*l*. there for rewardes att their despatrge., and to xlvij other persones xxviij*l*. ix*s*. viij*d*. late servauntes for their wages and rewardes of the Kinge's Majestie, as by a boke of the parcelles there may appere ... } xxxxviij*l*. ix*s*. viij*d*.'

Moulton Church before the Civil War

CHAPTER IV.

FROM EDWARD VI. TO WILLIAM III.

King's Commissions—Inventory of Moulton Church Goods, 1552—A Famous 'Mote Bell'—Resignation of Vicars—Reign of the Puritans—Destruction of Pinnacles and Spire—Cromwell and his Army, 15,000 Men, at Northampton—Loss of the 'Sanctus Bell' —New Bells, 1664—Later History, 1700—Description on an Ancient Bell at Moulton, *c.* 1230—Particulars of the Early Bells.

MANY and varied were the purposes for which Commissioners were appointed during Edward VI.'s reign—one for Church plate* and other valuables; another to search houses for Church property; a third ' to examine into the rents of the Crown estates, and to sell what remained of the chantry lands'; and, in addition to these, a special Commission was organized to collect bells, ornaments, and vestments.

On visiting Moulton in the year 1552, the Commissioners reported that there were in the tower six bells: a sanctus, four other bells, and a 'Mote-bell.' Some time previously, as appears from the inventory compiled in that year, 'the townspeople of Moulton, in

* The church plate at present consists of an elegant silver cup, 1607; a silver paten, *c.* 1685; and a silver bread-holder inscribed, 'The Gift of Mrs. Sarah Page to the Parish Church of Moulton, 1735.' All are well described in Mr. C. A. Markham's latest work—a volume of sterling worth, of engrossing interest—'The Church Plate of Northamptonshire,' 1894.

this county, purchased and set apart a special bell as a Mote-bell, which was to belong to the parishioners apart from the church. In the Inventory of Church Goods then belonging to that parish this bell is described as a " great bell " then hanging by itself in the bell-chamber, to be used as a clock-bell, and it was to be " ronge whan any casualtyes shall chaunce and for ye gatheryng togyther ye Inhabitants of ye sayd towne to ye Courte & other theyr necessaryes." '*

The period which followed was indeed a troubled one. Owing to the attitude of Henry VIII., Sir Thomas Farre (instituted March 13, 1542), and William Coxe (October 26, 1546) — both adhering to the Catholic religion — resigned the living. Christopher Browne (November 29, 1557), George Doxe (March 29, 1565), and William Dale (February 1, 1597) were successively inducted, but much bitterness fell to their lot.

Meanwhile the Puritans were becoming more powerful, and consequently more malicious, daily. About 1645 the spire was removed, and the beautiful pinnacles destroyed ; this was done, tradition would have us believe, by Cromwell's soldiers, who stripped off the lead with which it was covered, and turned it to good account—in other words, bullets for Naseby ! Tradition, however, is oft 'a lying jade,' and she has not been idle among the ruins of Boughton Parish Church—as usual, 'knocked down by Cromwell.' But in this case it is untrue, for the villagers, being unable to walk with comfort the three-quarters of a mile separating them from the church, allowed it to fall into decay at the beginning of the sixteenth century, and built for themselves a chapel in their midst ! Nevertheless Cromwell and his generals were in the locality both before and after the battle of Naseby, and from here he marched an army of 15,000 men into Worcestershire.

* North's 'Bells of Northamptonshire,' 1878, p. 339.

In the church itself the stained glass disappeared, and the chancel window was utterly destroyed. The sanctus-bell had previously been disposed of in some manner, and the rest of the peal damaged to some extent. In 1664 two new bells were placed in the tower; but these may have been two former bells having new inscriptions and dates, by reason of some unrecorded accident. Three bells, however, remain to be accounted for—whether broken, or sold, is not known.

Later, about 1700, there were five bells in the tower: the dates and inscriptions of the treble and second bells, however, are matters of uncertainty. The tenor had an interesting inscription in old Saxon capitals, which read as follows:

SANCTE CONFESSOR
CRISTI BENEDICTE ORA
PRO NOBIS DEUM.

The date of this bell is known to have been about 1230.* Other particulars concerning this early 'ring' may thus be stated:

Bell.	Date.	Diameter.			Weight.†		
		yd.	ft.	in.	cwt.	qrs.	lbs.
Treble	No date	1	0	1	9	0	12
Second	,,	1	0	3	11	1	3
Third	1664	1	0	6	13	3	12
Fourth	1664	1	0	10	17	3	7
Tenor	1216-72	1	1	7	27	0	0
		6	0	3	79	0	6

* See pages 36, 37, and 45, 46; North's 'Bells of Northamptonshire,' p. 340; Ellacombe's 'Bells of the Church,' p. 450.
† In the Churchwardens' Account Book the weight is erroneously given. It was not until April 24, 1895, that a copy of Mr. Arnold's bill was discovered.

CHAPTER V.

THE YEAR 1795.

Churchwardens' Accounts—Loyal Peals, Birthday of King George III.—Letters between Rev. W. Stanton and Mr. Edward Arnold—Last Occasion of ringing the Old Peal—The Curfew's Last Dirge.

THE five bells referred to in the last chapter were taken, in the year 1795, to Mr. Edward Arnold's foundry, Leicester, to be recast into a 'ring of six.' The entire weight amounted to 4 tons, considerably more than is shown by the Churchwardens' account book, in which an entry occurs for carriage at the rate of 8d. per cwt. Unfortunately, there are two items which appear to clash with each other. Here is the first:

	£	s.	d.
1795. Oct. 31. Pd. Mr. Aspinal for the Carriage of the Bells to Leicester, 46 cwt. and half at 8 pence ℔ cwt.	1	11	0

And here is the second, written by Clark Page Barber:

	£	s.	d.
1796. Apr. 17. Myself for the Carriage of the Old Bells down, and 3 of the New Bells up from Leicester, as ℔ Bill	3	16	4

No satisfactory explanation of the *double* charge has hitherto been accepted, and the items must, therefore, be doubtfully dismissed.

Although fears were long entertained as to the safety of

the bells, they were used for ordinary purposes until the day before they were lowered to the ground. June 4, 1795, is memorable, inasmuch as it was the last occasion on which a 'Loyal Peal' was rung. The entry in the account book runs:

	£	s.	d.
1795. June 4. Paid the Ringers Two Shillings being the King's Birth Day	0	2	0

Equally memorable, too, is the 'Loyal Peal' on King George III.'s birthday, June 4, 1796, since it was the first such peal rung on the new bells. To quote again:

	£	s.	d.
1796. July 4. Pd. the Ringers for the King's Birth Day the 4th of June last	0	2	0

On June 13, 1795, a letter was sent by the Rev. William Stanton, M.A., Vicar of Moulton, addressed to 'Mr. Edward Arnold, Bell-Founder, Hangman's Lane, Leicester.' Therein were stated the requirements of church and parish in the matter of bells, asking also for particulars with reference to their 'recasting.' In answer to this, the Vicar received a communication on the morning of June 19, stating that the founder would come over and interview both Vicar and bells; and this he did on July 2. Thirteen days later another letter was received (July 15), referring to the arrangements then in progress for the reception of the five bells.

July 19, 1795, was a day long to be remembered. Several times on that date were the bells rung, 'long and loud.' Hundreds of people, young and old alike, thronged the church, the churchyard, and the approaches thereto—some even climbing through the wide gap that had been prepared in the walls surrounding 'God's acre' to enable the tenor bell to begin its travels on the morrow. But the ringing was tinged with sadness, felt somewhat, by all; for were not they losing what to them, in that village community, was part of their existence? Were they not

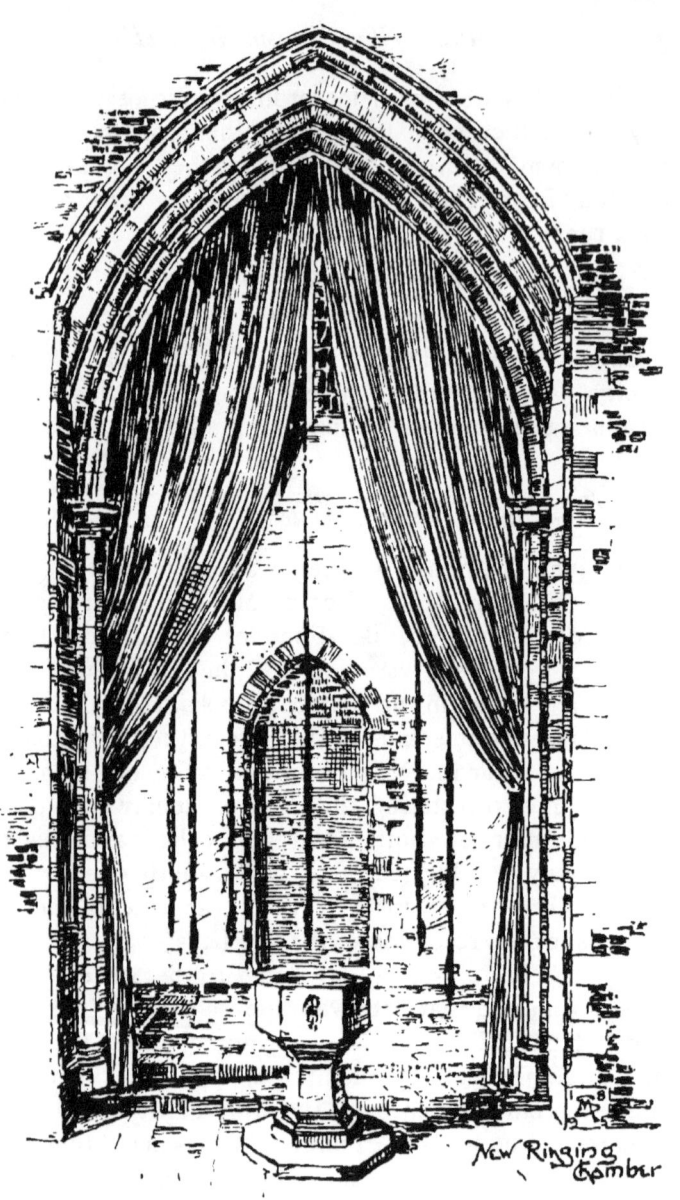

New Ringing Chamber

losing, too, what had so long shared their joys and griefs, their hopes and fears, and given strength and encouragement to them when in despair? Ay, what had guided them from their youth, had daily aroused them from sleep, proclaiming the hour for work, the time for rest, and the Benediction of the Church. How oft, indeed, had they heard 'the solemn sound of the passing-bell, calling upon all to offer a prayer for the departing soul of a neighbour—the death knell telling that all is over, that life's race is done—the funeral chime bringing calm in the midst of the heart's grief—the joyful peal announcing a birth, baptism, or marriage.' They remembered, and were sad. But none felt it as did the ringers themselves: the parting to them seemed strange and unaccountable—affecting, as ringers alone know.

* * * * *

Then the ringing ceased; and, for the last time, the Curfew tolled

'The knell of parting day.'

'Soft hour, which wakes the wish and melts the heart,
  Or fills with love the pilgrim on his way,
As the far bell of vesper makes him start,
  Seeming to weep the dying day's decay.'

BYRON.

CHAPTER VI.

ON THE ROAD: THE JOURNEY HOME.

Through Northamptonshire—Market Harborough reached—Leicestershire Route—At the Foundry—Contemporary Records—The Thirteenth-Century Tenor Bell, Inscription and Size—Analytical Tables of Route—The Welcome Home—Baptismal Ceremony—Particulars of the New Peal.

It was early on the morning of Wednesday, July 21, 1795, when the bells set out on their travels northward to Leicester, a distance by road of thirty-one miles. During the day they crossed many parishes—Boughton, Pitsford, Brixworth, Hanging Houghton, Lamport, Maidwell, Kelmarsh, Great Oxendon, and Little Bowden—and in the evening crossed the Welland, and drew up at the ancient inn of Harborough for the night. On the following day the journey was resumed, passing through Lubenham, Foxton, Smeeton Westerby, Kibworth Beauchamp, Kibworth Harcourt, Burton Overy, Great Glen, Oadby, and Knighton, until at length the bells arrived at the East Gate of the pleasant little town of Leicester, and proceeded to the bell foundry of Mr. Edward Arnold. Some particulars as to the route taken may be of interest:

WEDNESDAY, JULY 21, 1795.			THURSDAY, JULY 22, 1795.		
NORTHAMPTONSHIRE.			LEICESTERSHIRE.		
Parish.	Ascents.	Descents.	Parish.	Ascents.	Descents.
	ft.	ft.		ft.	ft.
1. Moulton*	82	88	11. Market Harborough	108	26
2. Boughton	20	22	12. Lubenham	51	7
3. Pitsford	46	127	13. Foxton	29	142
4. Brixworth	246	100	14. Smeeton Westerby	0	3
5. Hanging Houghton	105	29	15. Kibworth Beauchamp	118	6
6. Lamport	4	162	16. Kibworth Harcourt	79	122
7. Maidwell	234	69	17. Burton Overy	90	0
8. Kelmarsh	81	191	18. Great Glen	132	147
9. Great Oxendon	114	191	19. Oadby	45	167
10. Little Bowden	5	38	20. Knighton	43	141
	937	1,017		695	761

Three months elapsed, during which time the art of the bell-founder was skilfully employed in recasting the five old bells into a new peal of six—that Arnold was successful, all, who have since heard the fine peal, will readily admit. Among the visitors to the foundry was one of eminent authority in matters campanological. ' I may just observe,' wrote Dr. Throsby in 1795, 'that this year, a gentleman of considerable fortune came to Leicester purposely to see an old bell brought [from Moulton] to Mr. Arnold, bell-founder, to be recast. On it was the head of Henry III. [1216-1272], King of England at the time of Pope Benedict. Round the crown this:

'" Saunctie Confessor Christi Benedicte Ora Pro Nobis Devm."

. . . Its weight 27 cwt. Mr. Smith, the gentleman noticed above as a curioso in ancient bells, says there is

* A portion only; about a mile and a half.

only one of the same age that he knows of in England.'*
Some account of the history of this remarkable bell will
be given in a later chapter, however.†

On October 23, 1795, Friday, the return journey
was commenced, the bells being conveyed by a long team
of gray horses. Some idea as to the surface of the ground
traversed on this occasion may be conveyed by the following table :

County.	Miles.	Ascents. ft.	Descents. ft.	Greatest Rise.	Greatest Fall.	Highest Altitude.	Inclines Ascended.				
							Numb.	Under 40 ft.	Over 80 ft.	100 ft.	156 ft.
Leics.	15	761	695	114	108	447‡	23	18	5	3	—
Norths.	16	1,017	937	156	184	526§	38	31	4	4	1
	31	1,778	1,632				61	49	9	7	1

As on the first occasion, so now, a halt was made at
Market Harborough; and next day the journey came to
an end. Just outside the village, along the Pitsford
Road, the horses were brought to a standstill, whilst busy
hands bedecked the waggons with boughs of evergreen,
and the horses with ribbons. On again went the procession, the villagers singing and laughing with merry glee;
up the hill came the ponderous load—some pushing,
others running, skipping, jumping: what a goodly company! Soon they stopped, for the little inn‖ was reached.
Then commenced the profane 'christening.' In one of
the bells, which had previously been inverted, mine host
mixed 'a motley compound of beer, rum, etc.,' which was

* Thoroton's ' Hist. Notts.,' edit. Throsby, vol. ii., p. 88.
† See Chapter VIII.
‡ Kibworth Harcourt Manse.
§ Maidwell, near Brixworth.
‖ The Blue Bell, on Primrose Hill, so named from the proceedings here related.

liberally dispensed to the good-humoured bystanders. Of course the bell-founder was busy on this occasion, being provided with 'a more delicate mixture' in the treble with which to supply the distinguished persons in the company.* After the ceremony the bells were conveyed to the church and locked up for the night.

Particulars of the new peal may be conveniently arranged in tabular form :†

Bell.	Diameter.			Circumference.‡			Weight.			Note.
	yd.	ft.	in.	yd.	ft.	in.	cwt.	qr.	lbs.	
Treble	0	2	8½	2	2	6½	7	2	21	D
Second	0	2	10¼	2	2	11 9/14	8	1	4	C
Third	1	0	1	3	0	8¾	9	0	19	B♭
Fourth	1	0	3	3	1	2¼	10	1	8	A
Fifth	1	0	6	3	2	0	10	3	26	G
Tenor	1	0	9	3	2	9¾	17	0	8	F
	6	1	1¾	20	0	2 1/14	63	2	2	

* Rev. A. Gatty, *The Bell*, 1847.
† From actual measurements and calculations by the Author.
‡ Approximately true.

CHAPTER VII.

THE NEW PEAL, AND ITS SUBSEQUENT HISTORY.

Inscriptions on Treble and Tenor—Other Churches with same Mottoes—The Rev. William Stanton, M.A., 1738 to 1768—Memorial Tablet to the Stanton Family—Alterations and Restorations, 1816, 1818, 1847, 1848, 1849, 1853, 1855, 1878, 1880, 1883, 1884 to 1886—Vestry Regulations—The Church Clock and its Caretakers—The Chimers—Restoration of Tower and Bells, 1884—An Interesting Discovery—Mr. Arnold's bill for the bells.

WITH two exceptions, the inscriptions on the bells of Moulton are commonplace. The mottoes on the treble and tenor, however, are very suitable, and it is interesting to note the extent to which they have been adopted elsewhere.

The treble bears the following legend around its shoulders:

OMNIA FIANT AD GLORIAM DEI.

(Let all be done to the glory of God.)

This inscription was first used in Northamptonshire, among existing bells, in the year 1618, on the *tenor* of Helpstone Church; and last used, in 1795, at Moulton. The same motto occurs at the following places:

Date.	Church.	Bells.	Which Bell.	Weight.	Founder.
				cwt.	
1607	Paston	3	Treble	5¼	—
1610	Lutton	4	,,	4¾	—
,,	Pilton	4	3rd	6	—
1618	Elton (Hunts)	3	2nd	5½	—
,,	Helpstone	3	Tenor	6	R. S.
1629	Bulwick	5	Treble	6½	—
1732	Geddington	5	4th	8½	T. Eayre
,,	Kettering	8	6th	12	,,
,,	Raunds	6	3rd, 4th	9, 9¼	,,
1733	Benefield	5	4th	6½	—
1735	Achurch	4	Tenor	6	T. Eayre
,,	Oundle	8	4th	9½	,,
1738	Daventry	8	4th, 7th, 8th	6¾, 14½, 16¾	,,
1739	Wilbarston	4	Treble	5	,,
1742	Oundle	8	5th	11	,,
,,	Stanion	4	Tenor	7	,,
1744	Chelveston	5	Treble	4½	,,
,,	Oxendon Magna	4	Tenor	6	,,
1749	Boughton	3	,,	5	,,
,,	Easton-by-Stamford	4	3rd	7½	,,
1750	Little Bowden	3	Tenor	6½	,,
n.d.	Nassington	5	3rd	6½	,,
1783	Northampton, St. Giles	8	2nd	7	E. Arnold
1795	Moulton	6	Treble	6½	,,

At Moulton the tenor has this inscription :

> I TO THE CHURCH THE LIVEING CALL
> AND TO THE GRAVE DO SUMMONS ALL.
> E. ARNOLD, LEICESTER. FECIT 1795.

The couplet is inscribed also at Magdalen College, Oxford (1829), and at Sleaford (1796). In Northamptonshire this inscription appears to have been first used on the tenor of Wellingborough Parish Church (1639), and in the year following was added at Norton. Wollaston (1806) was the last addition made to the county. There are thirteen churches in Northamptonshire whose tenors have similar mottoes, varying slightly in form:

The New Peal, and its Subsequent History

Date.	Church.	Bells.	Weight of Tenor.	Founder of Tenor.
			cwt.	
1639	Wellingborough	6	26	—
1640	Norton	5	19	—
1682	Ringstead	6	14	M. Bagley
1683	Courteenhall	5	13½	H. Bagley
,,	Cransley	6	9¾	,,
1695	Bugbrooke	5	14	—
1700	Castor	6	9¼	H. Bagley
1708	Cotterstock	4	6½	H. Penn
1733	Northampton, Holy Sepulchre	6	15	T. Russell
1743	Floore	6	13	,,
1761	Earls Barton	6	13	T. Eayre
1795	Moulton	6	16	E. Arnold
1806	Wollaston	6	17	R. Taylor

Nor will it be out of place to refer to the Vicar whose name is immortalized by his deeds. The Rev. William Stanton was the son of a former Vicar of the same name, who held the living from 1738 to 1762. He was educated at Lincoln College, Oxford, and shortly after the death of his father was instituted at Moulton. He continued Vicar until 1830, being spoken of as 'the oldest incumbent in the county.' An interesting item appears in the Account Book of this period:—

'1831. Aug. 13. Paid Miss Dickens as per Bill for 120 Bows for the Sunday School Children for Mr. Wm. Stanton's funeral ... ... £ s. d. 0 8 0'

In the south chantry is a large inscribed slab, and also a mural tablet, which has a long inscription :

' Sacred to the memory of SARAH,
Daughter of the Reverend and Venerable JOHN CONANT, D.D,
Rector of Exeter College, Oxford, Regius Professor of
Divinity in that University,
Archdeacon of Norwich, Prebendary of Worcester, and Vicar of
All Saints', Northampton,
and Relict of the Reverend BENJAMIN KING, D.D., Vicar of
the said Church in Succession,
and Prebendary of Gloucester. Who died Sept. 15th, 1751.
Aged 93.

'Also of the Rev. WILLIAM STANTON, M.A.,
Many years Vicar of this Parish, and Rector of Bitteswell in the
County of Leicester.
And FRANCES his Wife, daughter of the above mentioned
BENJAMIN and SARAH KING.
He died June 7th, 1762, Aged 55 : She died Jan. 18th, 1769, Aged 64.

'Also of the Rev. WILLIAM STANTON, M.A., their Son.
62 Years the Resident and Officiating Vicar of this Parish, and
ELIZABETH his Wife ;
He died Sepr. 22nd, 1830, Aged 87 : She died Dec. 16th, 1830, Aged 85.

'Also of WILLIAM their Son, Scholar of Worcester College, Oxford.
Who died June 23rd, 1789. Aged 18.

'Also of GEORGE STAVELEY, who died in his infancy.'

Between 1795 and 1850 a few alterations and repairs were carried out. In 1818 this entry occurs :

'Sep. 1. Paid man for repairing the bells, 9
Days and Half at 6/6 per Day ... ... £3 1 9'

Again, in 1847, it was resolved at the Easter vestry 'that Mr. Pearson, of Northampton, be requested to examine the frames and brasses of the Bells, and that the Churchwardens be empowered to put them into good and substantial repair, after hearing his report.' The vestry also drew up regulations in 1848 and 1853 for the proper use and observance of the 'daily bells.' On November 9, 1849, an agreement was signed 'to give John Luck £3 10s. to repair the Church Clock; that he should put it in thorough repair, and unless it is done to the satisfaction of the parish he is not to receive the money ; to have new weights at the further expense of the parish ; also that the said John Luck be paid 7/6 per year to keep the clock in repair in future.'* The accounts showed that John Luck drew his instalments with commendable regularity! And yet again, April 13, 1855, did the vestry decide that 'the churchwardens be requested to ask for subscriptions for a new clock.' But the clock has not yet arrived. Indeed, the interest taken in the poor

* Minute book, November 9, 1849.

The New Peal, and its Subsequent History 43

old church 'timekeeper' is most pathetic! With regard to the ringers, the vestry decided on April 25, 1878, to pay them 'the sum of £2, and Mr. Britten the sum of £1 for attending to the Clock.' But the ringers murmured! Under April 5, 1880, is this entry: 'The chimers gave notice that they wished for an increase in their wages. Proposed . . . that the churchwardens see the chimers and make arrangements with them in regard to their application.'

The church tower was at this time in a deplorable state, and the bells, too, hung upon beams which threatened daily to give way. On November 15, 1883, a special vestry was held 'pursuant to notice duly given, to take into consideration the best means of raising funds to thoroughly repair the Church Bells, and appoint a Committee for that purpose. . . . Resolved: That the Bells be temporarily repaired, and put into order for the Christmas ringing.' The work was shortly afterwards carried out in a successful manner by Messrs. Taylor and Co., Loughborough. In reply to some questions, the firm courteously informed the Author that when the contract was executed 'the bells did not leave Moulton'; also, that 'entirely new framework and fittings were supplied for the six bells at a cost of £138 10s. in March, 1884. We do not know the exact weights of the bells,' they added. 'The treble is 2' 8½" in diameter, and the tenor is 3' 9", and probably weighs about 16 cwt.'* A

---

* Communicated by Messrs. Taylor and Co., bell-founders Loughborough, Leicester, January 8, 1895. A copy of Arnold's bill was discovered on April 24, 1895. The account is dated Oct. 30th, 1795, and reads thus: 'To a new Peel of Six Bells, weight 63 cwt. 2 qrs. 2 lb. ; Recd. 5 old Bells, wt. 79 cwt. 0 : 6. To recasting 63 cwt. 2 : 2, at 30s. per cwt., £95 : 5 : 6¼ ; Hanging Materials for the Six Bells, £42 ; Repairing and altering the frame £15 ; Six New Clappers, wt. 136¾ lbs. at 9d., £5 : 17 : 6¾ ; total, £158 : 3 : 1¼.' Against this is 'Allowed old Metal wt. 15 cwt. 2 : 4. at 8d., £58. Due to Balance £100 : 3 : 1¼ ; To six new Stays, Sliders, Screws, Bolts, etc., £3 3s., Men fixing the Clock, Hammer and other repairs, £1 1s. ; total, £104 : 7 : 1¼.'

'record' subsequently placed on the tower wall, near the font, commemorates the completion of this work: 'Moulton, Church of SS. Peter and Paul.—These bells were rehung by Messrs. John Taylor & Co., Loughborough, in 1884, at a cost of £138 10s.—Rev. O. R. Walker, *Vicar;* George Turner, Samuel Monk, *Churchwardens;* Robert York, *Superintendent.*'

An interesting discovery, which proved to be an ancient 'course' for four bells, was made during the restoration of the church in 1885-86. A small portion of this course, written on the woodwork of the ringing-chamber, was as below:

CHAPTER VIII.

LEGENDS THAT LINGER.

St. Andrews' Monastery Bells—Ruins of St. John Baptist Church, Boughton — Broughton Church mistaken — Cromwell's Mighty Deeds—Robbery in a Belfry—The Tenor Bell once more—Popes on the Scene, 1216 to 1272—Inventory of Bells at Boughton Parish Church—A 'Maiden' Bell at Moulton—Weston Favell Bells mistaken—Overstone and Sywell v. Moulton.

THE traditions relating to Moulton bells, though few in number, possess a certain amount of interest. The first relates that at the time of the dissolution of St. Andrew's Monastery, Northampton, two of its bells were transferred to Moulton Church.* There is certainly much to support the tradition, especially as the late Prior became Vicar in 1540; still, it is highly improbable, as shown in an earlier chapter.

It was in the sixteenth century, tradition would have us believe, that 'a party of Moulton people went secretly to the parish church of Boughton, stole a bell lying unhung in the tower, and brought it to their own parish.' Throsby, whose account of the ancient tenor bell is quoted elsewhere,† remarks of it: 'The history of this bell is this—that when Broughton Church, in Northamptonshire, was knocked down by Cromwell, the bell was taken to the

* Bridges' 'Northamptonshire,' vol. i., p. 419.
† P. 36, *ante.*

church of Moulton, near Northampton; thence brought to Leicester in 1795, to be recast with the rest of the Church Bells.' Mr. North, quoting and criticising this note, adds: ' Now, as Broughton Church was not "knocked down by Cromwell," and is, moreover, a considerable distance from Moulton, whilst Boughton is near at hand, there is, I think, little doubt that the bell in question came—if it did not originally belong to Moulton—from the latter place. This opinion is supported by the fact that the ancient church of Boughton, being a considerable distance from the village, was deserted in the sixteenth century, and allowed to fall into decay. It had two bells, one of which was broken down by thieves in the night and afterwards sold by the parishioners, and the second not unlikely, under the circumstances, found its way to Moulton."* Dr. Throsby, unfortunately, makes an error in his statement concerning the bell, viz.: ' On it was the head of Henry III., King of England, *in the time of Pope Benedict*,' for no such person upheld Papal supremacy 'during the reign of Henry III.' (1216-1272). The Popes during this period were:

1216.	Honorius III.	1265-9.	Clement IV.
1227.	Gregory IX.	1271.	Gregory IX.
1241.	Celestinus IV.		Innocent V.
1243.	Innocent IV.	1276 7.	Adrian V.
1254.	Alexander IV.		John XIX., or XX., or
1261.	Urban IV.		XXI.

But with regard to the tradition of 'stealing a bell from Boughton,' Throsby was evidently well aware of its existence. The performance was surely not a creditable one, if true! In the inventory of 1552, Boughton bells are thus referred to:

> ' It' too bellẽ of the which bellẽ the one was brocken don by theffes on a nyght cloffen & broken & then yt was sold by the holle co'sent of the piche unto Goodmā Freyre of Ecton for the some of v^{li} the whiche v^{li} was spēte in the defendynge of the Warren. It' one sanct' bell.'

---

* North's ' Bells of Northamptonshire,' 1878, p. 340.

One other tradition remains to be added: A belief has long been held that the present *fourth* bell (a 'maiden') was originally in the possession of the good people of Weston Favell, some three miles away, but that it was recast in 1795 with the remainder of the peal. This tradition is without the faintest tinge of truth!

Although not a legend but a reality, it would be a misfortune not to refer here to an interesting belief in 'Voices of Bells.' Every Sunday at 10.30 a.m., it is possible to hear the bells of Sywell, Overstone, and Moulton chiming together harmoniously. Then, according to a popular opinion, occurs this little dialogue:

SYWELL asks: 'Who rings best?'

OVERSTONE answers boldly: 'We do!'

But MOULTON cuts them short, exclaiming: 'No, you don't, for *we* do!!'

Interior of Original Belfry
From Photo by the Author 1894

CHAPTER IX.

PECULIAR USES AND CUSTOMS.

Chiming—Melodies—The 'Ave Maria'—General Uses. *Part I., Daily Bells:* Regulation, 1848 — (1) Harvest — (2) Spring and Summer—(3) Autumn and Winter—(4) Noonday—(5) Curfew. *Part II., Sunday Bells:* (6) Early Morning—(7) Second Hour—(8) Matins—(9) Conclusion of Service—(10) Sermon Bell, ii.—(11) Afternoon Service—(12) Sermon Bell, iii.—(13) Evensong. *Part III., Death Bells:* (14) Winding Bell—(15) Death Knell—(16) Infant's Passing Bell—(17) Funerals—(18) Dumb Peals. *Part IV., Miscellaneous Customs:* (19) Church Festivals—(20) Loyal Peals—(21) New Year's Eve—(22) Vestry Bell—(23) Induction—(24) Gleaning—(25) Plough Monday—(26) Execution of Charles I.—(27) St. George's Day—(28) St. Andrew's Day—(29) St. Paul's Day—(30) St. Stephen's Day—(31) Soulmas—(32) Lady Day—(33) Mote Bell—(34) Dole Meadow—(35) Apprentice—(36) Seed-sowing—(37) Harvest—(38) Sacrament Bell—(39) Sacring Bell.

THE 'Peculiar Uses and Customs' of the bells of Moulton Church are unusually interesting; most of them will be mentioned in this chapter. 'Chiming the bells' is at all times indulged in, and the following may often be heard just before the commencement of the evening service, on Sundays:

It was customary, also, on Lady Day, to chime as below, but this has not been done for several years now:

This 'melody,' repeated *ad libitum*, was undoubtedly the 'Ave Maria' of former generations.

The 'daily bells' are rung at 4 a.m. (Harvest), 5 a.m. (Summer), 6 a.m. (Winter), Noon, and 8 p.m. (Curfew); on Sunday, at 7 a.m., 8 a.m., 10.15 a.m. (Service), 12 (Noon Bell), 1 p.m., 2.30 to 3 p.m. (occasionally), 4 p.m. and 5.30 to 6 p.m. (Service).

PART I.—DAILY BELLS.

In the vestry minute-book an entry occurs regulating the daily bells: '1848. Easter Thursday. ... It was also proposed ... and seconded ... that the Bell should be rung at five o'clock in the morning instead of six, from Lady Day to the month of Harvest, and from after Harvest to Lady Day at six o'clock.'

I. 4 A.M.—The HARVEST BELL is probably the earliest-rung daily bell in the county. In 1893 it was first rung on the morning of Monday, July 31, and was continued daily for about five weeks.

II. 5 A.M.—The SPRING AND SUMMER BELL is rung an hour later than the Harvest Bell, from March 20 to September 22.

III. 6 A.M.—The AUTUMN AND WINTER BELL is commenced on September 23, and continued until March 19. In each case the third bell is used as the Seasons Bell.

IV. The NOONDAY BELL (third, but just as frequently the second bell) is rung daily at twelve o'clock. After the bell has been 'raised,' a pause is made, and then the hour of day is proclaimed by tolling *twelve* strokes at short intervals. A long pause follows, when the bell is again brought to its original position. This bell is silent on Sunday.

V. 8 p.m. — THE CURFEW.—This ancient institution still survives at Moulton. It is rung precisely at eight o'clock, both in summer and winter. Curiously, from time immemorial the Curfew has never been rung either on Saturday or Sunday evenings! Under date Easter, 1847, the vestry book records the desire 'that the ringing of the Church Bell at eight o'clock in the evening should be discontinued, and that it should be rung every morning except Sunday at six o'clock.' In the following year this entry occurs : ' It was also ordered that the Curfew Bell should be rung as usual in times past, [and] that 10s. per annum additional should be allowed the Parish Clerk for so doing.'

PART II.—SUNDAY BELLS.

None of the uses hitherto named are employed on Sunday; instead, the following customs are kept up with more or less regularity:

VI. 7 a.m. EARLY MORNING BELL. — This is one of the most interesting customs extant. It announces for the benefit of mankind the fact that at Matins a sermon will be preached; and for this purpose the second bell is used.

VII. 8 a.m. SECOND MORNING BELL.—An hour later two bells, third and fourth, are chimed for about a quarter of an hour; but the significance of this custom is not known.

VIII. MATINS.—Chiming the bells for this service now commences at 10.15 a.m., being continued until 10.40 a.m. ' Ringing in ' succeeds during the next five minutes, when the treble bell is usually used as ' *Ting-tang*.'

IX. The SERVICE-CONCLUDING BELL is another peculiar custom. Immediately the Benediction is pronounced, the second bell is rung as a notice to the villagers.

X. SERMON BELL, ii.—Should it be the intention of the Vicar to hold service in the afternoon, with sermon, the fact is proclaimed to the people two hours in advance by the ringing of the second and third bells at one o'clock.

XI. AFTERNOON SERVICE.—When held, the bells are chimed from 2.30 to 2.55 p.m., the 'ringing in' taking place during the next five minutes, as at Matins. It was formerly the custom to hold afternoon service every Sunday in the winter; but since 1885 this has not been done.

XII. SERMON BELL, iii.—At 4 p.m. it is the custom to chime the third and fourth bells for about fifteen minutes, in order to proclaim the tidings that a sermon will be preached at the evening service.

XIII. EVENSONG.—Chiming commences about 5.30 p.m., and lasts until 5.55, when the 'ringing in' again takes place. The bells, however, are just as frequently rung for this service.

PART III.—DEATH BELLS.

XIV. WINDING BELL.—This is the name given to the treble bell when rung immediately after the Noonday Bell; it proclaims that a funeral will take place in the afternoon of the particular day on which it is tolled.

XV. DEATH KNELL.—Having been acquainted of the person's decease, the clerk proceeds to inform parishioners by tolling the 'death bell' several minutes; after a time the bell is 'raised,' when the sex of the person is declared according to the formula:

> 'Thrice three tolls for a male,
> And thrice two for a female.'

XVI. INFANT'S DEATH KNELL.—A distinction is made in the case of a child. Instead of using the tenor bell, the third is employed; but 'sex' is denoted in the usual way.

XVII. FUNERALS.—The tenor is tolled for fifteen or

twenty minutes, and then 'raised' at the moment the funeral cortége is supposed to leave the house. This custom is peculiar to Moulton, and is often quoted by writers.

XVIII. DUMB PEALS are rung whenever a person of distinction dies. It has been customary also to pay the same tribute to the memory of a dead ringer. One of the most recent occasions was that at the death of Mr. John Dickens, who in 1810 rang with others a peal to celebrate the Jubilee of King George III. The present ringers brought him to the belfry with every care and kindness, in 1887, in order that, with assistance, he might likewise share the joys of Queen Victoria's Jubilee. He died at an age of nearly 100 years!

PART IV.—MISCELLANEOUS CUSTOMS.

XIX. CHURCH FESTIVALS are celebrated here right joyfully by merry peals throughout the day.

XX. LOYAL PEALS have been rung annually from time immemorial. The escape of King Charles on May 29 was formerly commemorated with much vigour by the villagers; for in addition to the clanging of bells, the tower was decorated with boughs of oak, and all observed high holiday. At present, peals are rung on May 24 and June 20—the birthday and coronation-day of our good Sovereign, Queen Victoria.

XXI. NEW YEAR'S EVE is observed in an interesting manner. At 11.30 p.m. the bells commence ringing a 'dumb peal,' and this is continued for half an hour; when midnight arrives *twelve* strokes are slowly tolled upon the Death Bell, and just as the last stroke is dying away, the whole peal suddenly breaks forth on the calm clear air.

XXII. VESTRY BELL, and XXIII. INDUCTION BELL. —Both are rung as occasion requires.

XXIV. The GLEANING BELL was rung at Moulton

Peculiar Uses and Customs 53

years ago, and several entries occur in the churchwardens' account-book for this purpose, from 1846 to 1852:

1846. July 31. Paid Walton Pell for crying the Gleaning ... ... 6d.
1852. Paid the Cryer to cry the gleaning ... ... 6d.

Among the customs formerly observed may be mentioned: Plough Monday, January 10; Execution of Charles I., January 30, 1648-49; St. George's Day, April 23; St. Andrew's, St. Paul's, and St. Stephen's Days; Soulmas and Lady Day; also the ringing of the Mote Bell; the Dole Meadow, Apprentice, Seed-sowing, Harvest and Gleaning Bells; and the Sacrament and Sacring Bells—but these are now, alas! the echoes of a forgotten past.

> 'And so 'twill be when I am gone,
> The tuneful peal will still ring on;
> While other bards shall walk these dells,
> And sing your praise, sweet *Moulton bells!*'

From Photo by
the Author 1894

Among the Bells

APPENDIX TO PART I.

I. VICARS OF MOULTON.

c. 1200. Budes.
? Thomas.
1263. Thomas de Ryhall, *priest*.
1280. Ralph de Stangoot, *chaplain*.
1287. Robert de Botelbrigge, *chaplain*.
1313. Reinold de Staumford, *chaplain*.
? Ralph de Lumleye.
? William de Brysingham.
1337. William de Welford, *priest*.
1348. Richard Gregory de Gauecote.
1353. William Mande Wolaston, *priest*.
1358. John de Wodeford, *priest*.
1373. Roger de Bromley, *priest*.
1404. Laurence Bozeate, *priest*.
? Thomas May.
1419. Sir John Verney, *priest*.
? Sir John Rame.
1433. William Potter.
1479. Master Thomas Allen, M.A.
1481. Sir Thomas Praty.
1482. Robert Eburton, *priest*.
1484. Sir John Alyson, *priest*.
? William Porter.
1530. Sir Henry Copinford, *chaplain*.
1540. Sir Francis Abree, S.T.P.
1542. Sir Thomas Farre, *clerk*.
1546. William Coxe, *clerk*.
1557. Christopher Browne.
1565. George Doxe, *clerk*.
1597. William Dale, *clerk*.
1607. William Fletcher, B.D.
1627. Thomas Campion, M.A.
1639. Edward Bagshaw, *clerk*.
Perkins ⎫
Hooke ⎬ *intruders*.
1660. Edward Bagshaw, *restored*.
1688. Joseph Birkhead.
1691. John Smith.
1730. William Knight, M.A.
1737. John Kay (died in June).

1737 (Sept. 9). William Stanton, M.A.
1762. William Thompson, LL.B.
1768-1830. William Stanton, M.A.
1836. Walter Poole, M.A.
1838. Thomas Sanders, M.A.
1878. Onebye Robert Walker, M.A.
1888. Alexander Mackintosh, M.A.
1892. William Holding.

II. TABLE SHOWING THE NUMBER OF VICARS INSTITUTED IN EACH CENTURY.

Century.	Vicars.	Century.	Vicars.	Century.	Vicars.
13th	5	15th	9	18th	5
14th	8	16th	8	19th	5
		17th	7*		

III. PRIORS† OF ST. ANDREW'S MONASTERY, NORTHAMPTON, WITH WHICH MOULTON WAS CONNECTED FROM 1084 TO 1540.

1176 (earlier). Robert Trianel; Abbot of Ramsey in 1180.
1180. Walter.
c. 1200. Samson.
? Ralph.
c. 1255. Robert de Winton.
c. 1256. William de Fonville.
1258. Guy; presented 9 kal. Feb.; resigned.
1270. John de Thifford; resigned.
1272. Bernard de Kariloco; presented by Convent de Caritate.
1288. Odo; presented 12 kal. Nov.
1293. Robert de Arcy.
1298. Bartholomew de Bosco; resigned.
1318. Guichar de Caroloco; Prior of Wenlock, 13 Edw. II.
c. 1332. William Conon.
c. 1343. Francis, a Fleming by birth; resigned.
1346. Thomas de Synarcleus.

* Including the two intruders.
† Dugdale's 'Monasticon Anglicanum,' vol. v.

c. 1358. Guy.
1387. John Dokesworth ; deprived.
1391. John de Tudenham.
c. 1399. Richard Napton.
c. 1452. John Holder ; died here, 1459.
1459. William Andrews (or Breknok).
1459. William Hamond ; resigned.
1490. Thomas Roche.
1503. Thomas York (or Skit, or Shere).
c. 1523. William Rekner.
c. 1538. John Petie.
c. 1538. Francis Abree (or Leycester) ; Vicar of Moulton, 1540 ; first Dean of Peterborough Cathedral, 1542.

IV. Carta ad Sanc^{TI} Andreæ Northamptonæ Prioratum Spectantes* — Respecting matters dealing with Moulton.

i. Carta Simonis primi Comitis.—[Ex. regist. S. Andreæ de Northampton penes Joh. Theyer de Conpershill juxta Gloucestr.] '. . . Et Grimboldus† dedit eisdem monachis in *Multonia* ecclesiam et totum decimam, et deciman Budonis, et terram unius carucæ. . . .'

ii. Carta Simonis Comitis, primi fundatoris.—[Ex. regist. S. And. in bibl. Hattoniana.] 'In Nomine summæ et individuæ Trinitatis, Amen. Notum sit sanctæ matris ecclesiæ filiis, quod comes Simon et uxor sua Matildis, ne in die judicii cunctis astantibus cum vacua manu appareant, largiti sunt de possessionibus suis monachis Sanctæ Mariæ de Caritate Deo apud Hamtonam in ecclesia sanctæ Dei genetricis Maria apostolique Andræ servientibus, pro animarum suarum salute, et omnium antecessorum suorum, necnon et dominorum et amicorum suorum et pro omnibus illis, qui locum istum auxerint, et hæc et alia ad ipsum locum pertinentia fideliter testificaverunt, ipsam ecclesiam Omnium Sanctorum . . . Grimboldus etiam dedit eisdem monachis in *Multonia* ecclesiam et totam decimam, et decimam Budonis, et terram unius carucæ, et Atardus suam decimam ; . . .'

* See Dugdale, vol. v., pp. 190-196.
† Lord of the Manor at Moulton.

iii. Confirmatio Donationum, per Hugonem Lincolniensem episcopam.—[*Ibid.*] 'Omnibus Christi fidelibus ad quos præsens scriptum pervenerit, Hugo Dei Gratia Lincolniensis episcopus salutem in Domino. Nostrum est justis petitionibus ad quiescere et quicquid possumus auxilii filiis sanctæ ecclesiæ impertiri ; unde et fratribus nostris monachis ecclesiæ sancti Andreæ de Northampton speciali authoritate qua fungimur confirmamus . . . Et ecclesiam de *Multon* cum omnibus pertinentiis suis.'

iv. Carta Regis Henrici primi donatorum concessiones ratificans.—[In registro S. And. de Northt. penes Joh. Theyer, fol. 14a. *Vide* Cart. 3 E. iii. n. 36 ; et Cart. 10 E. iii. n. 27.]. 'Henricus rex Angliæ Roberto Lincolniæ episcopo et David comiti et omnibus baronibus, et fidelibus suis, salutem. Sciatis me concessisse et dedisse monachis de caritate in ecclesia sancti Andreæ de Northampton. Deo servientibus, . . . in *Multon* duas virgatas terræ quas ipsi emerunt à Grimboldo, ita liberè tendneas sicut ipse tenet terram suam. Et ex dono ejusdem Grimboldi decimam de molendino, quod dicitur Cauchesmelne.'*

v. Valor Ecclesiasticus temp. Henry VIII.—[Return, 26 Hen. VIII., at First Fruits Office.] 'Prioratus Sc̄i Andree in Villa Northᵃmpton' P'dict'.—Frauncisc' Leicetert P'or P'oratus ib̄m. *Temp' al* Scitus P'orat' cum Terr' Dn̄icalibz . . . Reddit' in in div̄s' villis in com' Northt. Reddit' et Firm' in div̄s' al' villis et Hamlett' p annu', viz . . . *Molton* ad 2l. 4s. 6d. p annu' in manibz et usu' Thom' chipsey sibi concess' p p̄dc̄u' Wiłłm Rekner nup' p'orem p sigiłłm conventual' p timio annor' p deñiis de eod̄m Thom' metuat' d' quo quid̄m īmio adhuc restant 4ᵒʳ anni tamen hic dict' 2l. 14s. 6d. oñant 2l. 14s. 6d. . . .

 Penc̄ones in Com' Noʳhᵃmpt'.
  Penc̄one vicar' de *Molton* ... ... 0l. 13s. 4d.
  Et firm' rector de *Molton* ad 16l. p annu' concess'
   p p̄dēm Wiłłm Rekner nup' p'orem p'mio
   annor' Edwardo Watson et assignat' p deñiis
   ab eo metuat' d' quo quid̄m īmin' reman'
   4ᵒʳ ann' tamen hic oñant' ... ... 16l 0s. 0d.

* This mill is recorded in Domesday, and is still in existence.
† Vicar of Moulton, 1540.

vi. 'BOOK OF THE DEMAYNES OF THE LATE SUPPSSIDE HOWSE OF SAINT ANDREWS W{T}IN THE TOWN OF NORTH.'—[Augment. Office.] 'The terrar of all londs, as well arabill, pasture, as medeow, wiche were in the occupacion of the prior of Saint Andrews in Northt., being reputed and takin as the demeaines belonginge to the priory there, renuede at the survey of the kinge commyssioñs for the dissolucion of the sayd late priory this first day of Marche, in the xxix. Kinge Henry the viijth . . . ;' after which the return is recorded.

vii. CAPUT' MINISTRORUM DOMINI REGIS TEMP. HEN. VIII. —[Rolls 34 Hen. VIII. Augm. Office.] *Com' North'*.

	£	s.	d.
Hakylton, *Molton*, Syllyston—Firma tent' et terr.	0	13	4
	one ros' rub'		
Multon—Firma rectoria	10	0	0
Multon—Firma molend' aquatic'	2	13	4

viii. MISCELLANEA.—(*a*) Abstract of Priory Register in *Cott. Coll., Vesp. E. xvii.* 'No. 85, Cartæ de *Multon*, fol. 39.'

(*b*) Two bundles (Rolls—K. 7, and K. 8) in *Harleian Coll. MSS.:* both are imperfect—K. 8 being especially so. The first refers to *Moulton* under the title—'Computus Simon Dunstall receptoris domini Johannis Holder prioris prioratus sancti Andræ Northt. in comitatibus prædictis, videlicet defirmis, pensionibus, et porcionibus dicto prioratui spectan a crastino S. Michaelis Archangeli anno 34 Henry VI. usque in crast. ejusdem festi anno ejusdem regis 35 per unum integrum. . . .' The second is of fifteenth century date.

(*c*) *State of the Priory in* 1538.—'Dr Layton acquainted Cromwell, the visitor-general, by letter, 1538,* that "the house was in dett gretley, the lands sold and morgagde, the farmes let oute, and the rente recevide beforehande for x., xv., and xx. yeres, chaunter foundett to be paide oute of the londs, and grett bonds of forfeiture thereupon for non-payment." The same year the Prior and twelve monks surrendered the house by an instrument in English, printed in Weever's "Funeral Monuments," appendix, p. 106, and referred to in Burnet's "History of the Reformation,"

---

* Cott., Lib. Cleopatra, E. iv.

I. Ap., p. 149. See also Fuller's "Church History," book vi., p. 320.'

V. INVENTORY OF MOULTON CHURCH, 1552.

'Itm̃ iiij bellę & a sanct' bell.

'Itm̃ one other great bell hangyng in one frame by it selfe bought by Thomas Collę and Thomas Lucke And by yᵉ consent of yᵉ hooll pyshe for theyse causes folowyng (yᵗ is to say) to be yᵉ clocke bell and to have it ronge whan any casualtyes shall chaunce and for yᵉ gatheryng togyther yᵉ Inhabytantę of yᵉ sayd towne to yᵉ courte & other theyr necessaryes And not gyven to yᵉ sayd churche.'

VI. INSCRIPTIONS ON THE BELLS, 1795.

Treble: ✠ OMNIA FIANT AD GLORIAM DEI ✠ E. ARNOLD FECIT 1795

[Weight. 730 lbs; Diam. 2ft 9ins; Tone: D]

2nd: REVᴅ Wᵐ STANTON VICAR Wᵐ PELL MOULTON LODGE S CLARK PAGE BARBER. CHURCHWARDENS. 1795.

[Weight 840 lbs, Diam. 2ft 10½ins; Tone: C]

3rd: REVᴅ Wᵐ STANTON VICAR Wᵐ PELL MOULTON LODGE S CLARK PAGE BARBER. CHURCHWARDENS. E.A. FECIT 1795.

[Weight 1010 lbs; Diam 3ft 1ins; Tone: Bb]

4th: REVᴅ Wᵐ STANTON VICAR Wᵐ PELL MOULTON LODGE S CLARK PAGE BARBER CHURCHWARDENS. E A FECIT 1795

[Weight 1290 lbs; Diam. 3ft 3ins; Tone: A]

5th REVᴅ Wᵐ STANTON VICAR Wᵐ PELL MOULTON LODGE S CLARK PAGE BARBER CHURCHWARDENS. E. ARNOLD LEICESTER FECIT 1795

[Weight 1630 lbs, Tone: G; Diam.: 3ft. 6ins]

Tenor I TO THE CHURCH THE LIVEING CALL AND TO THE GRAVE DO SUMMONS ALL E. ARNOLD. LEICESTER. FECIT 1795.

[Weight 1800lb. Note F. Diam 3ft 9ins Circumf. of wheel 9 yds. The clapper is 4ft 2ins in length; its weight is probably 40 or 50 lbs. The tenor is also the clock bell and is struck by a hammer weighing about 12 lbs.]

*** Now that the Founder's bill has been discovered, the weights given above should be corrected. See pages 38, 43 and 60.

VII. Table of Weights and Diameters, etc., of the Old and New Peals.

Bell.	I. Weight.		II. Diameter.		III. Circumference.†	
	Ancient Peal.	Modern Peal.*	Ancient Peal.	Modern Peal.*	Ancient Peal.	Modern Peal.*
	lb.	lb.	in.	in.	in.	in.
Treble	1,020	861	37	$32\frac{1}{2}$	$116\frac{6}{7}$	$102\frac{1}{7}$
2nd	1,263	928	39	$34\frac{1}{4}$	$122\frac{3}{7}$	$107\frac{9}{14}$
3rd	1,552	1,027	42	37	132	$116\frac{6}{7}$
4th	1,995	1,156	46	39	$144\frac{4}{7}$	$122\frac{4}{7}$
5th	—	1,230	—	42	—	132
Tenor	3,024	1,912	55	45	$172\frac{6}{7}$	$141\frac{3}{7}$
Total	8,854 lb.	7,114 lb.	18 ft. 3 in.	19 ft. $1\frac{3}{4}$ in.	57 ft. $4\frac{2}{7}$ in.	60 ft. $2\frac{1}{14}$ in.

VIII. Table of the Distinctive Uses of Each Bell.

Bell.	Distinctive Uses.
Treble	Winding bell.
2nd	Noonday bell—Matins, conclusion of service—7 a.m. Sunday—priest's bell—1 p.m. Sunday.
3rd	7 a.m. Sunday, and at 1 p.m. and 4 p.m. same day.
4th	Harvest bell (4 a.m.)—Summer bell (5 a.m.)—Winter bell (6 a.m.)—Sunday, 8 a.m. and 4 p.m.
5th	Curfew—8 a.m. Sunday; sometimes at 4 p.m. on Sunday, when the preceding bell is likewise rung.
Tenor	Passing bell—Induction bell.

* From actual measurements by the Author, July 25, 1893.
† Calculated approximately.

IX. Table of Expenditure on Moulton Bells since 1778.

Items.	Period.	Years.*	Average. £ s. d.	Amount. £ s. d.
i. Ringing	1778-1893	96	1 19 9¼	190 17 6
ii. Bell-ropes	1778-1893	40	1 10 1½	60 4 8
iii. Re-casting Bells	1795	—	—	116 2 7
iv. Re-hanging „	1884	—	—	138 10 0
v. The Clock	1778-1893	72	1 5 7¾	92 6 8¼
vi. Miscellaneous	1778-1893	12	0 8 1½	4 17 7
				602 19 0½
	1778-1893	116	Average expenditure...	£5 3 11½

X. Extracts from Churchwardens' Accounts.

                                                                       £ s. d.

i. *Cost of the Present Peal:*

		£ s. d.
1795, June 19.	Pd. for a letter from Mr. Arnold the Bell Founder	0 0 4
July 2.	Expences for Beer, &c., with the Bell Founder	0 2 6
July 15.	Paid for a letter from Mr. Arnold the Bell Founder	0 0 4
„ 23.	Pd. Thos. Jeayes for repairing the churchyard wall as was taken down for the bells	0 1 9
„ 29.	Expences going to Leicester to weigh the bells	0 15 2
Aug. 20.	Pd. Postage of a Letter from Mr. Arnold the bell founder	0 0 4
Oct. 8.	Pd. for two letters from Mr. Arnold the Bell Founder	0 0 6
„ 21.	Pd. for a Letter from Mr. Arnold the Bell Founder	0 0 4

* The figures in this column are the actual numbers for which accounts have been recorded.

			£	s.	d.
Oct. 26.		Pd. for Oil for use of the New Bells	0	1	0
		Pd. Jno. Dickens going to Leicester with Mr. Clark Barber ...	0	3	6
,,	29.	Beer for the men about the Bells...	0	2	0
,,	31.	Pd. Mr. Aspinal for the Carriage of the Bells to Leicester 46 cwt. and half at 8 pence ᵱ cwt. ...	1	11	0
Nov.	5.	Beer for the Bell Men	0	1	0
,,	11.	Paid Mr. Edward Arnold for the New Bells, as ᵱ Bill	104	7	0
		Mr. Arnold's men for weighing the six new bells and the old Treble* Bell as ᵱ custom	0	7	0
		Henry Rabbut towards his expences and trouble with the Bells and Bell Founder	0	10	0
		Paid for a stamp for a receipt from Mr. Arnold	0	1	0
,,	16.	Paid for a new Lock for the Door atop of the Tower	0	1	6
,,	25.	Wm. Taylor for his Horse going to Leicester and twice to Northampton	0	5	0
		Mary Harris for a new set of Bell Ropes	3	10	0
1796, Apr.	17.	Myself [Clark Page Barber] for the Carriage of the Old Bells down, and 3 of the New Bells up from Leicester as ᵱ Bill	3	16	4
		To self for a Cart Rope as was cut to pieces taking the bells down	0	6	6

ii. *Concerning the Clock:*

1782, Oct. 23.	Paid Wm. Blunt for cleaning the Church Clock	0	2	6

* Weighed 9 cwt. 0 qrs. 12 lbs.

Extracts from Churchwardens' Accounts

		£	s.	d.
1785, May 12.	Paul Dodford for a Clock Line ...	0	9	0
1788, May 7.	Thos. Marriott for mending the Church Clock	0	1	0
1790, Feb. 16.	Paid Lee for Clock Work ...	0	12	0
June 4.	For taking down they Dyol Plate	0	1	0
	For shooteing the Clock Line ...	0	0	2
1791, Jan. 6.	Paid Tifield a Bill for Drawing & guilding the Dyol Plate ...	3	15	0
Apr. 27.	Paid John Blunt a Bill for they Dyol Plate...	3	1	0
June 18.	Paid a Bill for they Sun Dyol ...	0	5	0
1794, Feb. 14.	Wm. Lee Reparing the Church Clock	1	5	0
1796, Aug. 18.	Jno. Gross for reparing the Church Clock	0	1	0
1797, Mar. 25.	Mr. Lee for Reparing the Town Clock as ꝑ Bill	2	10	0
May 22.	John Tealby for fixing the hammer of the Clock	0	1	0
1799, Apr. 5.	For Shuting the Clock Line ...	0	0	6
1809, Feb. 9.	Lee for Cleaneing the Chirch Clock	0	10	6
1821, Sept. 22.	Paid Morgin as per Bill for 1 Clock Lin for the Parish Church of Moulton and for Blunt putin on	0	18	0
1850, Jan. 12.	Carriage of clock weights ...	0	1	0
Feb. 28.	Wm. Ogg, Church Clock Weights	0	16	4
Apr. 4.	J. Luck for repairing clock, &c. ...	3	10	0
1857.	Mr. Page for keeping the Clock in repair and winding up ...	1	10	0
1873, Nov. 11.	Mathews journeys to Brixworth with Church Clock	0	5	0
1876.	Bill for Gilding the Clock Face ...	0	15	0

iii. *Bell Ringing and Ringers:*

		£	s.	d.
1780.	Paid for 5 Ringing Daies (From 1778 to 1784, £4 4s. was expended for 42 'Ringing Days.' There are no such accounts recorded from 1785 to 1793.)	0	10	0
1794, June 4.	Paid the Ringers Two Shillings being the King's Birth Day	0	2	0
1796, July 4.	Paid the Ringers for the King's Birth Day the 4th of June last (These payments were made from 1794 to 1803, and 1807 to 1819. After 1796 the amount was increased to 3s.; altogether £5 3s. was paid.)	0	2	0
1809, Oct. 25.	Pd. the Ringers at the Jubilie	0	6	0
1837.	Britten, the Clerk, for ringing the bell	2	0	0
1869.	For ringing at Confirmation	1	0	0
1875.	Chimes	1	0	0
1876.	Paid the Chimers	2	0	0
1888, May 17.	J. Earl—Ringing at Confirmation	0	10	0
Dec. 18.	J. Earl—Ringing at Induction Service	0	15	0

There are no accounts recorded for twenty years in the period 1778-1895. Altogether nearly £200 has been spent for this purpose.

iv. *About Bell-ropes:*

		£	s.	d.
1778.	Paid for a new set of Bell roopes	1	6	0
	Spent when paid for the roopes	0	1	0
1791, Apr. 23.	Paid Dodfoard a Bill for they Bell Ropes and Clock Line	2	0	0
1794, Aug. 8.	Pd. Paul Dodford for a Sett of Bell Ropes	1	6	0

Extracts from Churchwardens' Accounts

		£	s.	d.
1796, July 24.	P^d. for a Cart Rope to mend the Bell Rop's ...	0	2	0
Oct. 28.	for a sit of Bell Ropes ...	1	16	0
1881.	Paid for Bell Ropes ...	1	10	0

v. *Miscellaneous Items*:

Here is the contract for a work of extraordinary magnitude!

1800, Oct. 9.	Oil for the Bells when Jno. Tealby was about them ...	0	0	2

And here, too, is the usual 'accompanying circumstance':

1800, Oct. 9.	Beer for ditto ...	0	0	3
1784.	Paid Wm. Blunt for mending the Bell Weels ...	0	3	6
1801, May 11.	Pd. Jno. Marriott for mending the Belfry Door key ...	0	0	8
1805, Oct. 8.	Pd. for Shooteing the Bell Rope ...	0	0	3
1818, Sept. 1.	Pd. Man for Repairing the Bells, 9 Days & half, at 6/6 per day ...	3	1	9
1825, Apr. 16.	Thos. Hayns for a new Brass for a Bell ...	0	9	6
1846, July 31.	Paid Walton Pell for Crying the Gleaning ...	0	0	6
1848, June 24.	New ladder for the Church [Belfry]	0	18	6
1846, 1849-52.	Paid the Cryer to cry the gleaning	0	0	6

PART II.

A SUMMARY OF NORTHAMPTONSHIRE BELLS,

With Extracts from Inventories, etc.

ABINGTON.—*4 Bells**: dated 1809, 1811, 1810 and 1764; in *1552*, 'iij bellẹ & a sanctes bell.'

ABTHORPE.—*1 Bell:* 1792. In *1552* 'ij bellẹ and a saunctẹ bell.'

ACHURCH.—*4 Bells:* 1861, 1675, 1711, 1735; *1552:* 'foure Belles in The Steple wyth a Sanct' Belle.'

ADDINGTON MAGNA.—*4 Bells:* 1807, 1807, 1605, 1630.

ADDINGTON PARVA.—*3 Bells:* 1610, 1620, 1629; *rehung* 1870.

ADSTON.—*1 Bell:* ? 1820; in 1700, none; in *1552*, 'one bell & a saunctẹ bell in the topp of the Churche.'

ALDERTON.—*5 Bells:* 1848, no date, 1670, 1848, 1670; *1552:* 'iij great bellẹ & a sanct' bell.'

ALDWINCLE, ALL SAINTS.—*5 Bells:* 1720, 1830, 1724, 1637, 1720; in *1700*, four bells.

ALDWINCLE, ST. PETER.—*3 Bells:* 1843, 1724, 1585.

APETHORP.—*4 Bells:* 1629, blank, 1671, no date; *1552:* 'iij Belles w^t a sanctis bell.'

ARTHINGWORTH.—*5 Bells:* 1695, 1775, n. d., 1598, 1589.

ASHBY ST. LEGERS.—*5 Bells**: 1641, 1630, 1806, 1630, n. d. (? 1600); in *1552*, 'ij bellẹ in ye steple & a sanct' bell,' and another bell sold at the time.

ASHLEY.—*5 Bells:* 1796, 1796, n. d., 1796, 1848; in *1700*, four bells.

ASHTON.—*5 Bells**: 1631, 1631, n. d., 1699, n. d. ; in *1552:* 'iij bellẹ a Sancts bell & ij hande bellẹ.'

ASHTON, near Oundle.—*1 Bell:* 1706.

ASHTON-LE-WALLS.—*4 Bells**: 1592, 1608, 1649, blank; *1552:* 'two bellẹ in the steple & A saunctẹ bell.'

* Including a priest's bell.

A Summary of Northamptonshire Bells

AYNHOE.—*9 Bells**: 1870, 1870, 1698, 1649, 1635, ? 1617, 1603, 1617, n. d.; *1552*: 'iiij bell℮ in y℮ stepull & a sanct' bell.'

BADBY.—*5 Bells*: 1623, 1623, 1754, 1623, 1822; *1552*: 'iiij great bell℮ in y℮ steple & a sanct' bell.'

BAINTON.—*4 Bells*: 1604, 1702, 1652, n. d.; *1552*: 'iij bell℮ in y℮ stepyH. one sanctus beH.'

BARBY.—*4 Bells*: 1621, n. d., 1605, 1625; *1552*: 'iiij bell℮ in y℮ steple & a sanct' bell.'

BARNACK.—*5 Bells*: 1715, 1608, 1609, n. d., n. d.; *1552*: 'iij bell℮ on lytyll handbell℮ of y℮ wch one is sold & the other stolen.'

BARNWELL, ST. ANDREW.—*2 Bells*: n. d., ? 1678.

BARNWELL, ALL SAINTS.—The 4 bells sold in 1821, when the church was taken down.

BARTON SEGRAVE.—*4 Bells*, which are ancient; no dates.

BENEFIELD.—*5 Bells*: 1713, 1755, 1847, 1733, 1815; *1552*: 'iij bellys.'

BILLING MAGNA.—*4 Bells**: 1684, n. d., n. d., 1664; *1552*: 'iij belles and a sanct' bell.'

BILLING PARVA.—*3 Bells*: cast circa 1850; *1552*: 'ij bell℮ and a sanct' bell.'

BLAKESLEY.—*6 Bells**: 1832, 1673, 1854, 1854, 1673, 1774; in *1552*, 'iiij bell℮ & a saunct℮ bell in the steple.'

BLATHERWYCKE.—*2 Bells**: n. d., 1685.

BLISWORTH.—*5 Bells*: 1758, 1624, 1624, 1713, 1758; *1552*: 'iij greate bell℮ and a Sanct' bell.'

BODDINGTON.—*6 Bells**: 1624, 1831, 1621, 1670, 1812, 1812; *1552*: 'iiij bell℮ in the steple & a saunct℮ bell.'

BOUGHTON.—*3 Bells*: 1824, 1824, 1749. The ancient church, in ruins now, possessed in *1552*: 'Too bell℮ . . . one sanct' bell.' In 1700 the three bells of the present church were dated 1653, and were the work of ' Henry Baglee.'

BOWDEN PARVA.—*3 Bells*: n. d., 1675, 1750.

BOZEAT.—*5 Bells*: 1723, n. d., n. d., 1635, 1635.

BRACKLEY.— i. ST. PETER: *5 Bells*, all dated 1628; *1552*: 'iij bell℮ in y℮ stepull & a sanct' bell.'
    ii. ST. JAMES: in *1552*, 'ij bell℮ in the steple & a sanct' bell.'
    iii. HOSPITAL CHAPEL: *1 Bell*, 1860.

BRADDEN.—*5 Bells*: 1701, 1703, 1701, 1701, 1832; *1552*: 'ij bell℮ & a saunct℮ bell in the steple.'

BRAYFIELD-ON-THE-GREEN.—*5 Bells*: 1699, 1732, 1699, 1676, 1676; in *1552*: 'iij grett belle—one sanct' bell.'

BRAMPTON ASH.—*6 Bells*: 1657, 1632, 1632, 1754, 1632.

BRAMPTON CHURCH.—*4 Bells*: 1628, 1616, 1607, 1616; *rehung* 1865.

BRAUNSTON.—*6 Bells:* 1811, all cast by Bryant; *1552:* 'iiij bellę in yᵉ steple & a sanct' bell.'
BRAYBROOK.—*4 Bells:* 1785, 1806, n. d., 1610.
BRIGSTOCK.—*5 Bells:* 1758, 1647 (last four).
BRINGTON.—*7 Bells*:* 1723 (six), priest's bell blank; in *1700:* five bells and a priest's bell (1614, 1613, 1616, 1637, 1670).
BRINGTON, ST. JOHN EVANGELIST.—*1 Bell:* 1856.
BRIXWORTH.—*5 Bells:* 1622, n. d. (? 1620), 1622, 1622, 1683.
BROCKHALL.—*3 Bells*:* Blank, 1609, blank.
BROUGHTON.—*5 Bells:* 1709 (first three), 1803, 1709.
BUGBROOK.—*6 Bells*:* 1863, 1868, 1599, 1813, 1695, 1813.
BULWICK.—*5 Bells:* 1629, 1629, 1630, 1859, 1648; *rehung* 1859.
BURTON LATIMER.—*5 Bells:* 1620, 1718, 1619, 1619, 1749.
BYFIELD.—*5 Bells:* 1703 (four), 1791; *1552:* 'iiij bellę in the steple & a saunctę bell.'
CANON'S ASHBY.—*1 Bell:* 1853; *1552:* 'iij great bellę in the steple.'
CARLTON, EAST.—*6 Bells:* 1755, n. d., 1755, 1660, recast 1755, 1755 (5th and 6th); in *1700,* four bells.
CASTLE ASHBY.—*5 Bells:* 1610, 1610, n. d., 1826 (5th and 6th); in *1700,* 6 bells.
CASTOR.—*6 Bells:* 1700; in *1552:* 'iiij grete bellys . . . a sanctus bell, two hand belles.'
CATESBY.—*1 Bell:* modern, date unknown; *1552:* 'iij bellę in yᵉ steple & a sanct' bell.'
CHACOMBE.—*6 Bells:* 1694 (four), 1790, 1863; *1552:* 'iiij bellę in yᵉ stepull & a sanct' bell.'
CHARWELTON.—*4 Bells:* 1844, 1844, n. d., 1630; *1552:* 'iij bellę in yᵉ stepl & a sanct' bell.'
CHELVESTON.—*5 Bells:* 1744, 1727, 1819 (3rd and 4th), 1727.
CHIPPING WARDEN.—*5 Bells:* all 1674; *1552:* 'iij bellę & a saunctę bell in the steple of A meane ryng.'
CLAPTON.—*1 Bell:* 1800; *1552:* 'iiij bellę in yᵉ stepull. It' ij hand bellę.'
CLAYCOTON.—*3 Bells:* 1810, 1615, 1619.
CLIPSTON.—*5 Bells:* 1752, 1599, 1681, 1589, 1869.
COGENHOE.—*3 Bells:* 1678, blank, 1678.
COLD ASHBY.—*3 Bells:* 1317, 1606 (2nd and 3rd); *1552:* 'In the steple ij bellę. Itm̅ a sanctus bell.'
COLD HIGHAM.—*4 Bells:* 1609 (1st and 2nd), 1663, 1609; *1552:* 'iij bellę in the steple & A saunctę bell.'
COLLINGTREE.—*4 Bells:* 1621 (1st and 2nd), n. d. (3rd and 4th).
COLLYWESTON.—*2 Bells:* 1636 (both); in *1548-9:* 'Itm̅ ij bellys in the steple. Itm̅ ij bellys takyne doune owt of the steple and sold;' in *1552.* 'ij bellę one gratt bell & a little bell. ij bellę takon downe.'

CORBY.—*4 Bells:* 1722 (all); in *1700*, three bells.
COSGROVE.—*5 Bells:* 1624, 1632, n. d., 1632, 1707; *1552:* 'iij bellę A sanct' bell & ij handbellę'; *1754:* 4 bells and 'a Saint's Bell in a small Turrit on the top of the Tower.'
COTTERSTOCK.—*4 Bells:* 1708; *1552:* 'iij bellę and j sanct' bell.'
COTTESBROOK.—*6 Bells:* 1702; *1552:* 'ffoure great bellę in the steple there & a sanct' bell.'
COTTINGHAM.—*6 Bells*:* 1704, 1790, 1704 (and 4th), 1865, n.d.
COURTEENHALL.—*5 Bells:* 1683; *1552:* 'iiij great bellę & a santes bell.'
CRANFORD, S. ANDREW.—*4 Bells:* 1718, 1624, 1683, 1624.
CRANFORD, S. JOHN.—*4 Bells:* 1629, Oct. 1717, 1663, 1857.
CRANSLEY.—*6 Bells:* cast in 1683; *rehung* 1870.
CREATON.—*4 Bells:* 1635 (3rd bell, 1636).
CRICK.—*4 Bells:* 1616, 1720, 1601, 1616.
CROUGHTON.—*4 Bells*:* 1679, 1629, 1703, n. d., ; *1552:* 'iij bellę in ye steple & a Sanct' bell.'
CULWORTH.—*6 Bells*:* 1712, 1747 (Dec. 23), 1806, 1612, 1636, blank; in *1552:* 'iiij bellę in ye steple & a sanct' bell.'
DALLINGTON, S. MARY.—*4 Bells:* 1688, 1598, 1713, 1625.
DALLINGTON, S. JAMES: a modern bell, by Messrs. Warner and Sons, London.
DAVENTRY, HOLY CROSS.—*8 Bells:* 1738 (6th: Oct. 29 ,1764); *weight*, 3 tons 13 cwt. 2 qrs. 16 lb. In *1552:* 'ij bellę in the steple & a sanct' bell ;' in *1700*, five bells: 1596, n. d., 1612, 1619, 1596 (weighing 2 tons 14 cwt., 3½ qrs.); *1743:* chimes added.
DAVENTRY, S. JAMES: modern, n. d.
DENS-HANGER.—*3 Bells:* circa 1870, small and unimportant.
DEENE.—*5 Bells:* 1832, n. d., 1862, n. d. (4th, 5th).
DENFORD.—*6 Bells:* 1629, 1581, 1680 (remainder).
DENTON.—*3 Bells:* 1827, 1625, 1629; in *1552:* 'iij bellę and one Sanctus bell.'
DESBOROUGH.—*5 Bells:* 1868, 1616 (2nd, 3rd), n. d., 1585.
DINGLEY.—*5 Bells:* 1785 (tenor, 1618); *1700:* four bells.
DODDINGTON MAGNA.—*5 Bells:* 1841; *1552:* 'thre bellę yn the steple wt a letle bell ;' *1700:* four bells.
DODFORD.—*6 Bells:* 1847, 1674, 1614, 1632, 1626, 1624; *1552:* 'iij bellę in ye steple & a sanct' bell.'
DRAUGHTON.—*4 Bells:* 1767; *1700:* one bell.
DUDDINGTON.—*1 Bell:* n. d., cast by Newcombe; *1700:* three bells.
DUSTON.—*3 Bells:* 1670, 1656, 1619.
EARLS BARTON.—*6 Bells:* 1720 (1st, 2nd), 1775, 1720 (4th, 5th), 1761; *1700:* five bells.
EASTON-BY-STAMFORD.—*4 Bells:* 1640, n. d., 1749, 1640; in

1552: 'ij great bellẹ & one little bell. It' ij bellẹ one broken & thother crakked.'

EASTON MAUDUIT.—*5 Bells:* 1663 (1st, 2nd), 1619, n. d., 1663.

EASTON NESTON.—*6 Bells:* 1771, 1846, 1823, 1771, 1820, 1823; in *1700:* four bells.

ECTON.—*6 Bells:* 1799, 1612 (2nd, 3rd), 1634, 1612, 1622; in *1690:* chimes added.

EDGCOTT.—*5 Bells*:* 1668, 1592, 1660, 1623, blank; *1552:* 'iij bellẹ in the steple of treble rynge & a sanctẹ belle.'

ETTON.—*3 Bells:* 1630, 1618 (2nd, 3rd); in *1552:* 'yn ye steple iij bellẹ & a sans Bell—one Sacrying Bell.—ij hand bellẹ.'

EVENLEY.—*6 Bells:* 1632, 1708, 1865, 1632, 1865, blank; *1552:* 'iij bellẹ in ye Stepull & a Sanct' bell.'

EVERDON.— *5 Bells:* 1625, 1635 (5th); *1552:* ' iiij bellẹ.'

EYDON.—*5 Bells:* 1770, 1822, 1795, 1603, 1872; *1552:* 'ij bellẹ in the steple & a saunctẹ bell.'

EYE.—*2 Bells:* 1712, 1866; *1552:* 'ij bellẹ. . one handbell.'

FARNDON, EAST.—*4 Bells:* 1675, 1710, blank, 1587.

FARTHINGSTON.—*5 Bells:* 1822, 1633 (2nd, 3rd, 4th), 1822; in *1552:* 'iij bellẹ in ye steple;' in *1700:* four bells.

FAWSLEY.—*4 Bells:* n. d. (16th cent.), same as in *1552:* 'iiij bellẹ in ye steple & a sanct' bell.'

FAXTON.—*2 Bells:* 1703.

FINEDON.—*6 Bells:* Recast 1825, 1875 (tenor); in *1700:* five bells.

FLORE.—*7 Bells*:* 1743, 1679 (2nd, 3rd), 1676, 1679, 1743, n. d.; in *1700:* five bells; *1800: bells rehung.*

FOTHERINGHAY.—*5 Bells*:* 1595, 1614, 1609, 1634, 1817; *1552:* 'iiij bellẹ in the steple ' and ' ij hand bellẹ.'

FURTHOE.—*1 Bell:* 1870; *1552:* 'Itm̄ one bell.'

GAYTON.—*6 Bells:* 1727, 1726 (remainder); *1821* (tenor recast); *1552:* 'iij bellẹ . . . of treble ryng And one small saynntẹ bell'; *1700:* '3 bells besides the Saints' Bell' (1585, 1594, 1662).

GEDDINGTON.—*5 Bells:* 1835, n. d. (2nd, 3rd: ancient), 1732, 1630.

GLAPTHORNE.—*3 Bells:* 1710, n. d. (2nd, 3rd); *1552:* 'iij belles' and 'ij hand belles.'

GLINTON.—*6 Bells:* 1799, 1798 (tenor); *1552:* 'fyrst in o^r stepylle iij belẹ. Itm̄ on sans bell. Itm̄ ij hand belẹ;' *1700:* five bells.

GRAFTON REGIS.—*4 Bells:* 1623 (1st. 2nd), n. d., 1839; *1552:* 'iij greate bellez and a Sant' bell.'

GRAFTON UNDERWOOD.—*4 Bells:* 1682; cast by Bagley.

GREATWORTH.—*4 Bells*:* 1825, n. d. (2nd, 3rd), 1707; *1552:* 'iij bellẹ in the steple & A saunctẹ bell;' *1700:* five bells.

A Summary of Northamptonshire Bells 71

GREEN'S NORTON.—*5 Bells:* 1810, 1757, 172⅞, 1829, 1727; *1552:* 'three belle & a sauncte bell;' *1700:* four bells.

GRENDON.— *5 Bells:* 1618, n. d. (2nd, 3rd), 1618, 1761; *1552:* 'iiij belle and a sanct' bell.'

GRETTON.—*6 Bells*:* 1761, 1636 (tenor); *1700:* four bells; rehung 1870.

GUILSBOROUGH.—*6 Bells:* recast 1847.

HADDON, EAST.—*5 Bells:* 1621 (1st, 2nd, 3rd), 1731, 1621.

HADDON, WEST.—*5 Bells:* 1636, 1611, 1682, n. d., 1729.

HANNINGTON.—*3 Bells*:* n. d., 1615, 1868.

HARDINGSTON.—*5 Bells:* 1669, 1871, 1682, 1669 (4th, 5th); *1552:* 'iiij grett belle & one sanct' bell brokyn.'

HARDWYCKE.—*1 Bell:* n. d. (ancient); *1700:* two bells. The first peal of *tubular bells*—8 in number—in Northamptonshire, dedicated August 16, 1894.

HARGRAVE.—*4 Bells:* 1603, 1748, 1675, n. d.

HARLESTON. —*6 Bells:* 1702, 1676 (2nd, 3rd, 4th), 1717, 1719.

HARPOLE.—*5 Bells:* 1834, 1725, 1635, 1782, n. d. (probably 1725); in *1700:* four bells (1628, 1618, 1635, 1678).

HARRINGTON.—*6 Bells:* 1817; *1700:* three bells.

HARRINGWORTH.—*6 Bells*:* 1805, 1603, 1805 (3rd, 4th), 1755, n. d.

HARROWDEN MAGNA.—*3 Bells:* n. d., 1629, 1715.

HARROWDEN PARVA.—*4 Bells:* 1624, 1732, 1624 (3rd, 4th).

HARTWELL.—*1 Bell:* 17th cent.; in *1552:* 'ij belle . . . on handbell goode stolen.—Itm̃ on off owre belle stolle.'

HAZLEBEACH.—*4 Bells:* 1621.

HELIDON.—*4 Bells:* 1635 (tenor, 1615); in *1552:* 'iij belle in yᵉ steple & a sanct' bell;' *bells rehung* 1860.

HELMDON.—*7 Bells*:* 1797, 1855, 1834, 1679 (4th, 5th, 6th), n. d. (priest's bell); in *1552*. 'iiij belle in yᵉ stepull & a sanct' bell.'

HELPSTON.—*3 Bells:* 1671, 1866, 1618; *1552:* 'iij belles. Item in the same steple one little belle. Item tow handbelles.'

HEMMINGTON.—*4 Bells:* 1872, 1724, 1598, n. d.; in *1552:* 'ij belle & a sanct' bell . . . a hand bell.'

HEYFORD.—*4 Bells:* 1638, 1601, 1704, 1601.

HIGHAM FERRERS.—*7 Bells*:* 1820, 1633, n. d. (3rd, 4th), 1636, 1633, 1660 (p. b.).

HINTON-IN-THE-HEDGES.—*3 Bells*:* n. d. (1st, 2nd), blank (p. b.); *1552:* 'iij belle . . . & a sanct' bell.'

HOLCOT.—*3 Bells:* 1703, n. d. (broken), c. 1610.

HOLDENBY.—*2 Bells:* 1719; in *1600* there were six bells.

HOLLOWELL.—*1 Bell:* about 1840, the church being modern

HORTON.—*3 Bells:* n. d. (1st, 2nd), 1641; in *1549:* 'ij Greate bellę & a broken—A Sanctę bell.'
HOUGHTON MAGNA.—*2 Bells:* n. d., 1817; *1552:* iiij greate bells and one sancte bell'; *1700:* five bells.
HOUGHTON PARVA.—*5 Bells:* 1720, 1669, 1624, 1685 (4th, 5th).
IRCHESTER.—*6 Bells**: 1846, 1729, n. d. (3rd, 4th), 1792, n. d. (p. b.).
IRTHLINGBOROUGH.—*6 Bells:* 1829.
ISHAM.—*4 Bells:* 1626, 1619, n. d., 1615.
ISLIP.—*5 Bells:* 1678 (tenor, 1621).
KELMARSH.—*6 Bells:* 1774; in *1700:* four bells.
KETTERING, S. PETER.—*8 Bells:* 1714 (1st, 2nd), 1860, 1714, 1630, 1732, 1722, 1832; in *1700:* five bells; *clock* added 1756.
KETTERING, S. ANDREW.—A modern bell (? 1880).
KILSBY.—*4 Bells:* 1706 (1st, 2nd), 1616, 1625; *1552:* 'iij bellę in yͤ steple & a sanct' bell.'
KINGSCLIFFE.—*5 Bells:* 1714, 1619, 1832, 1592, 1738; *1552:* 'iij belles wᵗ a sanctus bell.'
KING'S SUTTON.—*9 Bells**: 1793 (1st, 2nd), 1722, n. d., 1626 (5th, 6th), 1655, 1602, 1738 (p. b.); *1552:* 'iiij bellę in yͤ steple & a sanct' bell whereof j is sold;' *1700:* six bells.
KINGSTHORP.—*5 Bells:* 1621, 1680, 1621, 1622, 1671; *1552:* 'iiij bellę and a sanct' bell.'
KISLINGBURY.—*5 Bells:* 1799, 1659, 1733, 1659 (4th, 5th).
LAMPORT.—*5 Bells**: 1872 (1663), 1641 (2nd, 3rd), 1616, blank (p. b.).
LAXTON.—*1 Bell:* 1822; *1700:* three bells.
LICHBOROUGH.—*4 Bells**: 1876, 1628, 1753, 1835 (p. b.); *1552:* 'iij bellę in yͤ steple & a sanct' bell & one bell sold.'
LILBOURNE.—*5 Bells:* 1762 (1st, 2nd, 3rd), n. d., 1761; *1700:* four bells (1626, n. d., n. d., 1658).
LOIS WEEDON.—*4 Bells:* n. d., 1705 (remainder); *1552:* 'iij bellę & a sauncte bell.'
LODDINGTON.—*3 Bells:* 1803; in *1700:* four bells.
LONG BUCKBY.—*5 Bells:* 1814 (treble), 1624 (2nd to 5th).
LONGTHORPE.—*1 Bell:* unknown; *1552:* 'an olde crackyd bell.'
LOWICK.—*5 Bells:* n. d. (1st, 2nd), 1713, n. d., 1619.
LUDDINGTON.—*2 Bells:* 1710.
LUTTON.—*4 Bells:* 1610, 1682, 1604, 1619; *1552:* 'iij gret bells & one saunctus bell. It' ij handbells.'
MAIDFORD.—*2 Bells:* 1625, 1663; *1552:* 'ij bellę in the steples & a saunctę bell.'
MAIDWELL.—*5 Bells:* 1772 (Sept. 18); *1700:* four bells.

A Summary of Northamptonshire Bells 73

MARHOLM.—*1 Bell*: 1673; *1552*: 'ij bellę & a sans bell yn yᵉ steple.'
MARSTON TRUSSEL.—*5 Bells*: 1612, 1622, 1621, 1622, 1623.
MARSTON, S. LAWRENCE.—*5 Bells*: 1627, n. d. (2nd, 3rd), 1627, 1639; *1552*: 'iiij bellę in yᵉ stepull & a sanct' bell.'
MAXEY.—*6 Bells*: 1853, 1800, 1661 (3rd, 4th) 1800, 1661; *1552*: 'iij bellę & a lyttull bell.'
MEARS ASHBY.—*4 Bells*: 1793, 1621, n. d., 1718.
MIDDLETON CHENEY.—*7 Bells**: 1671, 1659, 1680, 1693, 1651, 1640, 1810 (p. b.); *1552*: 'iiij bellę . . . & a sanct' bell.'
MILTON MALSOR.—*5 Bells*: 1686; cast by Bagley.
MORETON PINKNEY.—*5 Bells*: 1629; *1552*: 'iiij great bellę & a sanctę bell.'
MOULTON.—*6 Bells*: recast by Arnold, 1795; *1552*: 'iiij bellę & a sanct' bell . . . one other great bell;' *1700*: five bells (1st and 2nd unknown; 3rd and 4th, 1664; tenor, 1216-1272).
NASEBY.—*5 Bells*: 1633, 1640, 1633 (3rd to 5th).
NASSINGTON.—*5 Bells*: 1874, 1686, n. d., 1642, 1801; *1552*: 'fowre belles.'
NEWBOROUGH.—*2 Bells*: 1828.
NEWBOTTLE.—*2 Bells*: Blank, 1660; *1552*: 'iij bellę — & a sanct' bell.'
NEWNHAM.—*6 Bells*: 1660, 1633, 1632 (3rd, 4th), n. d. (5th, 6th); *1552*: 'iij bellę . . . & a sanct' bell.'
NEWTON BROMSWOLD.—*3 Bells*: 1746, n. d., 1639.
NEWTON-IN-THE-WILLOWS.—*1 Bell*: 1806.
NORTHAMPTON, ALL SAINTS.—*8 Bells*: 1782; *chimes* added 1829.
NORTHAMPTON, S. EDMUND.—*8 Bells*: presented (? 1884) by the churchwarden, W. Tomes, Esq., Mayor of Northampton, 1894-5.
NORTHAMPTON, S. GILES.—*8 Bells*: 1783; in *1700*: six bells; *rehung*, 1895.
NORTHAMPTON, S. PETER.—*8 Bells*: 1734; *1700*: four bells.
NORTHAMPTON, THE HOLY SEPULCHRE.—*6 Bells*: 1739, 1681, 1857, 1681, 1805, 1733.
NORTHAMPTON, S. ANDREW (1842), S. KATHARINE (1839), S. CRISPIN, S. LAWRENCE, S. MARY (Far Cotton), S. MATTHEW (Kingsley Park), S. MICHAEL AND ALL THE ANGELS, S. PAUL, etc.—Each has a modern bell, dating from the erection of the church.
NORTHBOROUGH.—*2 Bells*: n. d., 1611; *1552*: 'ij small belles . . . A sanctę belle . . . one handbelle.'
NORTON.—*5 Bells*: 1640; *1552*: 'iij bellę in yᵉ steple & a sanct bell.'

OAKLEY MAGNA.—*4 Bells**: 1626, n. d., 1634, n. d. (p. b.).
OAKLEY PARVA.—*1 Bell*: 1833.
OLD.—*5 Bells*: 1825, 1723, 1631, n. d., 1639.
ORLINGBURY.—*5 Bells*: 1843; *1700*: three bells.
ORTON.—*1 Bell*: 1775.
OUNDLE.—*8 Bells*: 1868-9 (1780), same, 1868-9 (1688), 1735, 1742, 1763, 1801, 1868-9 (1748); *1700*: six bells.
OVERSTONE.—*2 Bells*: 1609, 1676; *1700*: four bells; *1552*: 'iij bellę and a Sanct' bell.' The ancient church, however, was pulled down in 1803.
OXENDON MAGNA.—*4 Bells*: 1820 (?), n. d., 1853, 1744.
PASSENHAM.—*5 Bells*: n. d., 1711, 1624, 1585, 1817 (1635); *1552*: 'iiij grett bellys and one Sanct' bell.'
PASTON.—*3 Bells*: 1607, n. d., 1601; *1552*: 'iij belles — A sanct' belle.'
PATTISHALL.—*6 Bells**: 1631 (1st, 2nd), 1609, 1630, 1770, 1713 (p. b.); *1552*: 'iiij bellę & a sаunctę bell in the Steple.'
PAULERSPURY.—*5 Bells*: n. d., 1654, 1623, n. d., 1613; *1552*: 'fyve bellę one sanct' bell ij handbellę.'
PEAKIRK.—*2 Bells*: n. d., 1677; *1552*: 'ij smale bellę — on handebell.'
PETERBOROUGH, THE CATHEDRAL.—*5 Bells*: 1709 (1st to 3rd), 1831, 1709. Henry Penn cast *ten Bells* in the year 1709, but five were sold in 1831.
PETERBOROUGH, S. JOHN BAPTIST.—*9 Bells**: 1808, 1675 (p. b.); in *1552*: 'v Great bellę yn the styple and one saunctus bell one hand bell v sacryng bellę.'
PETERBOROUGH, S. MARK (1856), S. PAUL (1868), S. MARK, and other modern churches have but *one bell*.
PIDDINGTON.—*5 Bells*: 1845, 1845-6, 1846, 1845-6 (4th, 5th); *1552*: 'iij bellę'; *1700*: six bells.
PILTON.—*4 Bells*: n. d., 1610 (2nd, 3rd), n. d.; *1552*: 'iiij belę & a sanct' bell.'
PITSFORD.—*5 Bells*: 1698, n. d., 1632 (3rd to 5th); *1552*: 'iij bellę wᵗ a sanctus bell.'
PLUMPTON.—*2 Bells**: 1678, blank (p. b.); *1552*: 'ij lyttle bellę & a saunctę bell.'
POLEBROOK.—*5 Bells*: 1717, n. d. (2nd, 3rd), 1771, 1765; *1552*: 'foure bellę . — . a sacrnge bell.'
POTTERSPURY.—*5 Bells*: 1774, n. d., 1792, n. d., 1625; *1552*: 'v beilę and a sanctus bell.'
PRESTON CAPES.—*5 Bells*: 1829, 1631 (2nd to 5th); *1552*: iiij . bellę . — . & a sanct' bell.'
PRESTON DEANERY.—*1 Bell*: 1710; cast by Henry Penn.
PYTCHLEY.—*5 Bells*: 1621, 1618, n. d., 1622 (4th, 5th).

A Summary of Northamptonshire Bells 75

QUINTON.—*2 Bells:* 1682, 1719; *1552:* 'ij Greate bellę and a sanct' belle.'

RADSTON.—*2 Bells:* n. d.; same as in *1552:* 'ij littill bellę.'

RAUNDS.—*6 Bells:* 1732, 1723, 1732 (3rd to 6th); *1700:* 5 Bells.

RAVENSTHORPE.—*5 Bells:* 1809; *1720:* three bells (1627, n. d., 1712).

RINGSTEAD.—*6 Bells:* 1682; cast by Bagley.

ROADE.—*4 Bells:* 1721, n. d. (2nd to 4th); *1552:* 'iiij bellę & one Sanct' bell.'

ROCKINGHAM.—*1 Bell:* 1776.

ROTHERSTHORPE.—*4 Bells:* 1638, 1719, 1630, 1638; *1552:* 'three bellę and one sanct' bell.'

ROTHWELL.—*6 Bells:* 1682 (1st—3rd), 1860, 1726, 1857.

RUSHDEN.—*6 Bells:* 1794 (tenor, 1818).

RUSHTON.—*5 Bells:* 1720, 1732, 1844, n. d., 1598.

SCALDWELL.—*4 Bells:* 1621, 1682, 1621 (3rd, 4th).

SIBBERTOFT.—*5 Bells:* 1825, recast; *1700:* three bells.

SILVERSTON.—*1 Bell:* 1655.

SLAPTON.—*3 Bells*:* n. d.; *1552:* 'ij bellę — & a saunctę bell.'

SLIPTON.—*1 Bell:* 1846.

SOUTHWICK.—*2 Bells:* Blank, n. d.; *1552;* 'two belles a bygger and a lesser.'

SPRATTON.—*5 Bells:* 1685; *1552:* 'iij bellę and a sanctus bell.'

STAMFORD BARON.—*6 Bells:* 1850; *1552:* 'iij grete bellę and a little bell.'

STANFORD.—*6 Bells*:* 1631, 1624, 1605, 1640, 1631, blank (p. b.)

STANION.—*4 Bells:* 1607, n. d., 1742, n. d.

STANWICK.—*3 Bells:* n. d., 1721, 1613.

STAVERTON.—*5 Bells:* 1726, 1776, 1662, 1720, 1776; *1552:* 'iij bellę.'

STEANE.—None; but in *1552* there was 'one lyttil bell.'

STOKE ALBANY.—*5 Bells:* 1790; Taylor's S. Neots Foundry.

STOKE BRUERNE.—*5 Bells:* 1684 (1st, 2nd), 1770 (3rd, 4th), 1684; *1552:* 'iiij bellę and a sancktus bell.'

STOKE DOYLE.—*5 Bells:* 1727; *1552:* 'iij great bells & a lytle bell.'

STOWE-NINE-CHURCHES, S. MICHEL.—*4 Bells:* 1725, 1790, 1607 n. d.; *1552:* 'iij bellę in yᵉ steple & a sanct' bell.'

STOWE-NINE-CHURCHES, S. JAMES.—*1 Bell:* c. 1856.

STRIXTON.—*1 Bell:* 1671.

SUDBOROUGH.—*4 Bells:* 1647, blank, n. d., 1647.

SULGRAVE.—*6 Bells*:* 1759, 1610 (2nd, 3rd), 1744, 1806, blank (p. b.); *1552:* 'iiij bellę — & a saunct' bell.'

SUTTON.—*1 Bell:* 1867, J. Warner and Sons, London; *1552:* 'ij smale belles — a sanct' bell. Itm̃ ij handbells.'
SUTTON BASSETT.—*1 Bell:* 1718; *1700:* two bells.
SYRESHAM.—*5 Bells:* 1624 (1st, 2nd), 1687, 1624, 1867; *1552:* 'iij bellę in yᵉ steple & a sanct' bell.'
SYWELL.—*3 Bells:* 1701 (?), 1766, 1611; *1700:* four bells.
TANSOR.—*3 Bells:* n. d., 1611, n. d.; *1552:* 'iij bellę j sanct' bell & j hand bell.'
THENFORD.—*5 Bells:* 1731, n.d., 1737, 1601, 1806; *1552:* 'iij bellę in yᵉ stepull & a Sanct' bell'; *1700:* three bells.
THORNBY.—*5 Bells:* 1714 (tenor, 1844).
THORNHAUGH.—*3 Bells:* 1619, 1634, 1860; *1552:* 'iij bellę & a sans bell. It' ij hand bellę sold.'
THORPE MALSOR.—*6 Bells:* 1860, 1680 (2nd, 3rd), 1751, 1817, 1680.
THORPE MANDEVILLE.—*3 Bells:* 1790, 1636, 1826; *1552:* 'ij littill bellę in yᵉ steple & a sanct' bell.'
THRAPSTON.—*5 Bells:* 1686, 1765, 1677, n. d., 1634; *1552:* 'iiij bellys — And a sacryng bell.'
TICHMARSH.—*6 Bells:* 1688 (1st, 2nd), 1781, 1688 (4th, 5th), 1708.
TIFFIELD.—*3 Bells:* 1764, 1809 (2nd, 3rd); *1552:* 'iij bellę.'
TOWCESTER.—*6 Bells:* 1725, 1626 (2nd to 4th), n. d., 1823 (June 13); *1552:* 'iiij bellę & a sauntcę bell in the steple whereof one is sold.'
TWYWELL.—*3 Bells:* 1867, n. d. (2nd, 3rd).
UFFORD.—*3 Bells:* 1670, n. d. (2nd, 3rd); *1552:* 'one handbell —iij bellę & a lytle belle.'
UPTON (near Peterborough).—*1 Bell:* n. d.; *1552:* 'ij small Bellę — on' handbell.'
UPTON.—*2 Bells**: n. d., blank (p. b.); *1700:* three bells.
WADENHOE.—*3 Bells:* 1603, n. d., 1607.
WAKERLEY.—*3 Bells:* 1598, 1663, 1599; *1700:* four bells.
WALGRAVE.—*6 Bells**: 1867, 1723 (2nd, 3rd), 1766, 1723, n. d. (p. b.).
WANSFORD.—*2 Bells:* 1868, n. d.; *1552:* 'ij bellę yn yᵉ steple wᵗ a sans bell. It' ij hand bellę wᵗ a sacryng bell.'
WAPPENHAM.—*4 Bells:* 1865, 1618, 1599, 1610; *1552:* 'iij small bellę.'
WARKTON.—*3 Bells:* 1718, 1761, 1638; *1700:* four bells.
WARKWORTH.—*2 Bells:* 1740 (March 25), 1841; *1552:* 'ij bellę in yᵉ stepull & a sanct' bell.'
WARMINGTON.—*5 Bells:* 1670, 1669, 1604, 1710, n. d.; *1552:* 'Itm̃ one bell clapper & small gynnes belongyng to a chyme. It' ij sacrynge bellę stolne.'
WATFORD.—*6 Bells:* 1695, 1712, 1695 (3rd to 5th), 1820 (recast).

A Summary of Northamptonshire Bells 77

WEEDON BEC.—*5 Bells:* 1745 (1st, 2nd), 1665, 1624, 1822; *1552:* 'iiij bellẹ in yᵉ steple & a sanct' bell.'
WEEKLEY.—*5 Bells:* 1832 (1st, 2nd), 1771, 1615, 1628.
WELDON.—*6 Bells:* 1710; Henry Penn founder.
WELFORD.—*5 Bells:* 1699, 1859, 1633 (3rd, 4th), 1638.
WELLINGBOROUGH, PARISH CHURCH.—*7 Bells*:* 1640, 1604, 1729, 1764, 1620, 1639, 1708 (p. b.). At the several daughter churches, one bell.
WELTON.—*5 Bells:* 1823, 1629, 1825, 1629 (4th, 5th); *1552:* 'iij bellẹ in yᵉ steple & a sanct' bell.'
WERRINGTON.—*2 Bells:* Blank; *1552:* 'ij bellẹ and a sanctus bell.'
WESTON-BY-WELLAND.—*5 Bells:* 1865 (1st, 2nd), 1616, 1598, 1662.
WESTON FAVELL.—*5 Bells:* 1683 (tenor, 1707); *1552:* 'iij bellẹ and a sant' bell.'
WHILTON.—*6 Bells:* 1777; *1700:* 3 bells.*
WHISTON.—*5 Bells:* 1729, 1611, n. d., 1635, 1638; *1552:* 'one great bell—It' one sanctus bell.'
WHITFIELD.—*5 Bells:* 1870 (1st, 2nd), 1869, 1870 (4th, 5th); *1700:* three bells; *1552:* 'ij littill bellẹ in yᵉ steple.'
WHITTERING.—*3 Bells:* 1681, n. d., 1681; *1552:* 'iij bellẹ and a lyttyll bell. It' ij handebellẹ.'
WHITTLEBURY.—*4 Bells:* 1694, 1634, n. d., 1628; *1552:* 'iij bellẹ . . . & a saunct' bell.'
WICKEN.—*6 Bells*:* 1620, 1798, 1620, 1619 (4th, 5th), 1686 (p. b.); *1552:* 'iij smalle bellẹ . . . ij hand bellẹ.'
WIKE-HAMON likewise possessed 'ij bellẹ off iij weyght by estymatyō.'
WILBARSTON.—*4 Bells:* 1739, 1704 (2nd, 3rd), 1639.
WILBY.—*3 Bells:* 1705, 1682, n. d.
WINWICK.—*3 Bells:* n. d.; treble by Edward Newcombe.
WOLLASTON.—*6 Bells:* Blank, 1806, 1868, 1806 (4th, 5th, 6th).
WOODFORD.—*5 Bells:* 1616, 1673, 1662, 1839, 1616.
WOODFORD HALSE.—*4 Bells:* 1613; *1552:* 'iiij bellẹ . . . & a saunctẹ bell.'
WOOD NEWTON.—*2 Bells:* 1640, 1720; *1552:* 'iiij bells wᵗ a littill bell.'
WOOTTON.—*5 Bells:* 1770, 1629, 1660, 1620, 1836; *1552:* 'iij great bellẹ and a [sanct'] bell.'
YARDLEY HASTINGS.—*6 Bells:* 1723; 'Henry Penn, Fovnder.'
YARWELL.—*3 Bells:* n. d., 1714, 1754; *1552:* 'ij bellẹ.'
YELVERTOFT.—*5 Bells:* 1634; the tenor is inscribed:

ℭum ℭum and Praise

PART III.

BIBLIOTHECA CAMPANALOGICA

Sec. I. Foreign Works: 1416 *et seq.*

1. Alcuinus, A. F.   Opera de Divinis Officiis. *Paris,* 1617, fol.
†2. Anon.   Recueil curieux ed édifiant sur les cloches de l'église, avec les cérémonies de leur Bénédiction. *Cologne,* 1757.
3. Anonymous.   Essai sur le Symbolisme de la Cloche. *Poictiers,* 1859, 8°.
*4. Arnoldus, Heinricus.   [8°. *C.* 179. *Linc.*] Exercitium academicum de Campanarum usu.   *Altdorf,* 1665, 8°.
5. Barbosa, Augustinius.   Duo vota consultiva de Campanis et de Cœneteriis.   'Quamquis tantum libellus tamen rarissimus.'   *C.* 1600, 4°.
6. Baronius, Cæsar.   De Ritu consecrandi Campanas, in decimo tomo Annalium.   *Romæ,* 1858.
7. Barraud, Abbé.   Notice sur les Cloches.   *Caen,* 1841, 8°.
8. Bernardus, Gulielmus.   Axiomata quædam deque Sepulturis et Exequiis.   *Paris,* 1547, 8°.
9. Beyerlinck, Laurentius.   Magnum Theatrum humanæ vitæ sub vocibus Campana, Tintinnabulum, etc., fol.   *Colon.,* 1631.
10. Bierstaldt, A.   Dissertatio Historica de Campanarum materia et forma.   *Jenæ,* 1685.
*11. Billon, J. B.   [1743, *e.* 8.]   Campanologie: étude sur les cloches et les sonneries françaises et étrangères par M. le docteur Billon: avec une notice biographique par C. Vasseur.   *Caen,* 1866, 8°.
12. Boehmerus, G. L.   Programma de Feudo Campanario. *Gottingæ,* 1755.

† For the Bodleian copy of this work, see No. 17.
* Subject Catalogue, Bodleian Library, Oxford.

13. BUOMMATTEI, B.   Declamazione delle Campane dopo le sue Cicalate delle tre Sirocchie. *Pisa*, 1635.
14. CANCELLIERI, F.   Descrizioni della nuova Campana magiore della Basilica Vaticana. *Romæ*, 1786.
*15. ——— Le duc nuove campane di Campidoglio; con varie notizie sopra i campanili, etc. [1, Δ. 1038.] *Romæ*, 1806, 4°.
*16. CAPUA, G. DI, CAPECE. [1743, *d.* 9.] Dissertazione di Giuseppe di Capua Capece intorno alle due campane della chiesa . . . di S. Giovanni de Nobilo Vomini di Capua . . . alla quale si dà principio conaltra dissertazione sopra lo stesso argomento di P. M. Paciaudi. *Napoli*, 1750 (*fours*), 8°.
*17. CARRE, R. [55, *c.* 64.] Recueil curieux et édifiant sur les cloches de l'église, avec les ceremonies de leur Bénédiction. *Cologne*, 1757, 8°.
18. CAVE, G. G.   Au Turrium et Campanarum Usus in Repub. Christ. Deo displiceat. *Leipsiæ*, 1790, 4°.
19. CAVILLIER, PH.   Œuvre campanale, ou le Fondeur familier. *n. pl.*, 1750.
20. CONRAD, D.   De Campanis Germanice. *n. pl. or d.*
21. CORBLER, J.   Notice Historique et Liturgique sur les Cloches. *Paris*, 1857.
22. ——— Note sur une cloche fondue par Morel de Lyon. *Paris*, 1859.
23. D'ARCER.   Instruction sur l'Art le separer le cuivre du métal des cloches. *Paris*, 1794, 4°.
24. DERFELDE.   Dissertatio de Origine et Nomine Campanarum. *Jena*, 1685.
25. D'IVERNOIS, R.   La Voix des Cloches dans l'Eglise, discours par. *Neufchatel*, 1867.
26. DERGNY, M. D.   Les cloches de Pays de Bray. *Paris*, 1866.
27. DEVORA, H. R.   Uber dis Erfindung Gesprungene Clocken. *Ouedlingburgh*, 1821, 12°.
28. DIETERICUS, C.   De Campanis. *n. pl. or d.*
29. DRABICIUS, N.   De Cœlo et Cœlesti Statu. *Metz*, 1618.
30. EGGERS, N.   Dissertatio de Origine et Nomine Campanarum. *Jenæ*, 1683.
*31. ——— Diss. de campanarum materia et forma; resp. A. Bierstädt. [*Diss.*] *Jenæ*, 1685, 4°.
32. ELLIS, SIR RICHARD.   Commentarius de Cymbalis. *Rotterodami*, 1727, 8°.
33. EMDENII, J.   Von rechter Einweihung der Glocken. *Neuhus.*, 1634.

34. ESCHENWECKER, T. M. De eo quod justum est circa Campanas. *Halæ*, 1708, 4°.
35. FEILNERI, J. Turcken Glocke. *Leipsic, n. d.*
36. FELIX, LE R. P. La Voix de la Cloche. *Paris*, 1869, 12mo.
37. FESC, L. DU. Des Cloches. *Paris*, 1607-19, 12mo.
*38. FISCHER, J. P. A. [1743, *d.* 8.] Varhandeling van de klokken en het klokke-spel. *Utrecht*, 1738, 4°.
39. FUSCHI, P. De Visitatione et Regimine Ecclesiarum. *Romæ*, 1581, 4°.
40. GAGUINUS, R. Annales Francorum. *Paris*, 1514.
41. GOEZIUS. Diatriba De Baptismo Campanarum. *Lubecæ*, 1612.
42. GRIMAUD, G. Liturgie Sacrée, avec un Traité des Cloches. *Lyons*, 1666, 4°.
43. ——— *Paris*, 1686, 12mo.
44. GUACCIUS, F. M. De Sonitu Campanarum. *n. pl. or d.*
45. HAHN, J. G. Campanologie. *Erfurt*, 1802, 8°.
46. HERMANSEN, J. De Baptismo Campanarum. *Holm*, 1728, 4°.
47. HERRERA, P. A. Del Origen y progresso de Officio Divino. *n. pl. or d.*
48. HILSCHEN, G. Diss. de campanis Templorum. *Leipsiæ*, 1690.
49. HOMBERGIUS, G. De Superstitiosis Campanarum pulsibus, ad cliciendas preces, quibus placentur fulmina, excogitatis. *Frankfortiæ*, 1572, 4°.
50. ——— Responsio de superstitione campanarum pulsibus, quibus placentur fulmina. *Frankfortiæ*, 1577.
51. HOSPINIANUS, R. De Templis. *Geneva*, 1672, fol.
52. Irenius Mentanus Historic. *Shemniz*, 1726.
53. Isei Ku Chac Chung. *n. pl. or d.*
*54. JACOB, V. [1743, *d.* 4.] Recherches historiques sur la tour et la cloche de Mutte de la cathedrale de Metz. *Metz*, 1864, large 8°.
55. KATZSEY. Notizen über Glocken, 2 vols. *Cologne*, 1855, 8°.
56. LAMPE, F. A. De Cymbalis veterum. *Traj. ad Rhen.*, 1703, 18mo.
57. LANE, J. G. Au Turrium et Campanarum usus Deo displiccat. ? *Leipsiæ*, 1704, 4°.
*58. LANGLOIS, E. H. [1743, *d.* 2.] Hymne a la cloche. *Rouen*, 1832, 8°.
59. LAUNAY, C. Der Glockeniësser. *Leipsiæ*, 1834.
60. ——— Manuel de Fondeur. *Paris*, 1854, 18mo.
*61. LAZZARINI, A. [8°. Σ., 514.] De vario tintinnabulorum usu apud veteres Hebræos et ethnicos, 2 vols. *Roma*, 1822, 8°.

62. LINDNER, J. G. De Baptismo Campanarum. *n. pl. or d.*, 4°.
*63. LUDOVICI, J. F. [*Diss. B.* 113, *L.* 20.] Diss. de eo quod justum est circa campanas; resp. J. M. Eschenwecker. *Habæ*, 1708, 4°.
*63a. ———— ed. alt. [*Diss. P.* 104.] *Habæ*, 1739, 4°.
*64. MAGIUS, HIERONYMUS. [8°. *B.* 10, *Jur. Seld.*] De tintinnabulis, cum notis Franc. Swertii. *Hanov.*, 1608, 8°.
64a. ———— ed. alt. aucta, emendata, et figuris æneis exornata. *Amst.*, 1664, 8°.
64b. ———— ed. alt. acc. ejusdem majii de equules liber, cum notis G. Junger-manni. [i. *Crynes.* 173; ii. *Douce. M.* 160.] *Amstelodami*, 1689, 8°.
64c. ———— p. 1157, vol. ii. Nov. thesaur. alb. Henr. de Sallengre. *Hagæ. Com.*, 1724, fol.
65. MAIOLUS, S. Dies Caniculares, h.e. Colloquia. *Unsellis*, 1600, 4°.
*66. MATTEINI, D. M. [1743, *e.* 12.] Dono al S. Padre Pio ix. [Beginning: 'Il sacerdote D. Mariano Mattcini. ... 26 Octob., 1869, offri al S. Padre un campanello tutto a trafori da se idea to e lavorate di sua mano.' With a photograph of the Bell.] *Rimini*, 1869 (*two*), 4°.
67. MODELIUS, J. G. An Campanarum Sonitus Fulmina, Tonitura, et Fulgura impedire possit. *Chemu.*, 1703, 4°.
68. MITZLER, B. A. De Campanis. *n. pl. or d.*
69. MONTANUS, J. Nachricht von den Glocken, deren Ursprung, nutzen Gebrauch. *Chemnitz*, 1726, 8°.
*70. MONTFERRAND, A. R. [1743, *a.* 1.] Description de la grand cloche de Moscow. *Par.*, 1840, *large fol.*
71. MORAND, M. F. Inscriptions et Noms d'Ancienne et de la Novelle Clocke du Beffroi de Boulogne sur Mer. *n. pl.*, 1841.
72. MOREL DE VOLEINE, L. De la Sonnerie des Cloches, dans le Rit. Lyonnois. *Paris*, 1860, 8°.
*73. MORILLET, L. [1743, *d.* 15.] Etude sur l'emploi des clochettes chez les anciens et depuis le triomphe du Christianisme. *Dijon*, 1818, large 8°.
74. NERTURGII, M. Campanula Pœnitentiæ. *Dresden*, 1644, 4°.
*75. NOLIBOIS, J. [1743, *e.* 10.] Notice sur les Cloches de Saint-Michel de Bordeaux, sa construction primitive, de 1472 à 1492; sa restauration de 1860 à 1869. *Bordeaux*, 1869, 8°.
76. NUES VRA, SENORA DEL PUCHE. Camera Angelica de Maria Santissima. *n. pl. or d.*
77. OTTE, H. Glockenfunde. *Leipsic*, 1858, 8°.
78. PACIAUDI, P. M. Dissertazione su due Campane di Capua. *Neapoli*, 1750, 4°.

*79. PACICHELLIUS, J. B. [*Douce, P.* 549.] De tintinnabulo Nolano lucubratio autumnalis. *Neapoli,* 1693, 8°.
80. PAGII. De campanis dissertatio. *n. pl. or d.*
*81. PARDIAC, J. B. [1743, *e.* 9.] Notice sur les cloches de Bordeaux et en particulier sur celle de l'église Notre-Dame (extrait du Bulletin monumental publ. à Caen). *Paris (Caen),* 1858, 8°.
82. PYGIUS, A. De pulsatione campanarum pro defunctis. *n. pl. or d.*
*83. QUIÑONES, JUAN DE. [1743, *e.* 14.] Discurso de la Campana de Villila in Diocesi Cæsaraustana in Hispania. *Madrid,* 1625, 4°.
*84. REIMANNUS, J. C. [*J.J.* 48. *Jur.*] Dissertatio philologico-philosophico-juridica, de campanis earumque origine, vario usu, abusu, ac juribus ex varus auctoribus conscripta et elaborata. *Isnaci,* 1679, 4°.
*84a. ——— Diss. de campanis earumque origine, vario usu, abusu, ac. juribus. [*Diss. N.* 10.] *Isnaci,* 1694, 4°.
85. Relatione sopra il Toccamento della Campana de Viliglia, Romæ. *Rome,* 1652, 4°.
86. RHODIGINUS, L. C. Lectionum Antiquarum Libri. *Venet.,* 1416, fol.
87. RESENIUS, P. J. Inscriptiones Haffniensis. *Hafniæ,* 1668.
*88. ROCCA, SEU ROCCHA, SEU ROCCHENSIS (ANGELOS) CAMERS, SEU DE CAMERINO, EPISC. FAGAST. [i. 4°. *R.* 5. *Th. Seld.;* ii. *Douce, R. R.* 116.] De campanis commentarius. *Rom.,* 1612, 4°.
*88a. ——— Col. 1233. Vol. II. Sallengre novi thes. *Hagæ Com.,* 1718, fol.
89. ROUJON. Traité des Harmoniques et de la Fonte des Cloches. *Paris,* 1765, 8°.
90. SALLENGRE, A. H. DE. Thesaurus Antiquitatum Romanarum. *Venice,* 1735, fol.
91. SAPONTI, G. M. Notificazione per la solenne Benedizione della nuova campana de Collocarsi nella Metropolitana di S. Lorenzo. *Geneva,* 1750.
*92. SAUVAGEOT, C. [1743, *d.* 3.] Etude sur les cloches; lettre à Didron, directeur des 'Annales archéologiques.' *Paris,* 1863 (*fours*), large 8°.
*93. SCHÆPKENS, A. [1743, *e.* 7.] Des cloches et de leur usage (Extrait de *La Belgique,* Sep., 1857). *Bruxelles,* 1857, 8°.
94. SCHIEFERDECKER, J. D. De ritibus convocand : ad sacra. *Cirzæ,* 1701, 4°.
*95. SCHOETTGEN, C. [*Diss. I.* 63.] Diss. de nolis in vestitu ad illustrationem verborum hymni sacri : und die schollen Klingen, etc. ; resp. E. F. Kürschner. *Stargard,* 1725, 4°.

96. SECQUET, J. M.   Observations sur la Métal des Cloches. *Paris*, 1801, 8°.
97. SELIGMANN, G. F.   De Campana Urinatoria. *Leipsiæ*, 1677, 4°.
98. SPIERS, R. P.   Tractatus Musicus Compositoris Practicus. *Augsburgh*, 1746.
*99. STOCKFLETH, H. A.   [*Douce, S.* 343.]   Diss. de Campanarum usu. *Altd.* 1665, 8°.
100. STORIUS, G. M.   De Campanis Templorum. *Leipsiæ*, 1692, 4°.
101. STRAETEN, E. V.   Notice sur les Carillons d'Audenarde. *n. pl. or d.*
*102. STRAUB, M. L'ABBÉ A.   [1743, *d.* 5.]   Notice sur les deux Cloches Anciennes d'Obernai (extrait de *La Revue catholique de l'Alsace*. Dec., 1859. *Strasbourg*, 1860, large 8°.
103. STURMIUS.   De Campana Urinatoria. *n. pl. or d.*
*104. SULZBERGER, H. G.   [1743, *e.* 13.]   Sammlung aller thurganischen Glockeninschriften sammt einer einleitenden Abhandlung über die Kirchenglocken; mitgetheilt von H. G. Sulzberger. . . . [Thurganische Beiträge Fur vaterländischen Geschichte herausg. vom histor. Vereine des Kantons Thurgau Heft. 13.)   *Frauenfeld*, 1872, 8°.
105. THIERS, G. B.   Des cloches. *Paris*, 1602, 1619, 12mo.
*106. THIERS, J. B.   [i. 8°. *Z.* 135 ; ii. *Douce, T.* 202.]   Traïtez de Cloches, et de la sainteté de l'offrande du pain et du vin aux messes des morts, non confondu avec le pain et le vin qu'on offroit sur les tombeaux. *Paris*, 1721, 8°.
107. THURGANISCHE, B.   See 104 *super*.
108. VERGERIUS, P.   De origine, Campanarum. *n. pl. or d.*
*109. VILLEMARQUÉ, LE VICOMTE HERSART DE LA.   [1743, *d.* 6.]   Mémoire sur l'inscription de la cloche de Stival près Pontivy, en Bretagne.   [Extrait du tome xxiv., IIe. partie, des Mémoires de l'Académie des Inscriptions et Belles-lettres. *Paris*, 1864, 4°.
*110. VOLEINE, L. MOREL DE.   [1743, *e.* 11.]   De la sonnerie des cloches dans le rit lyonnais.   [Extrait du *Journal la Mâitrise*.] *Paris*, 1860, 8°.
111. WALLERI, A.   De campanis et præcipius earum usibus. *Holmiæ*, 1694, 8°.
*112. WICHTIGE ERFINDUNG.   [1743, *f.* 3.]   Ueber die wichtige Erfindung, gesprungene Glocken. *Ouedlinburg*, 1821 (*eights*), 12mo.
113. WILLIETTI, C.   Ragguaglio delle campane di Viliglia. *Romæ*, 1601, 4°.

114. WION, A. De campanarum usu. *n. pl.*, 1665, 12mo.
115. ZEHE. Historiche Notizen uber des Glockengiekerfund. *Munster*, 1867, 8°.

SEC. II. ENGLISH WORKS: 1668-1895

*116. ACLAND-TROYTE, CAPT. J. E. [*Gough Adds. Eccles. Top.*, 8vo., 29.] The change-ringers' guide to the steeples of England. *Lond.*, 1879; *2nd ed.*, 1882, 8vo.
*117. ALPHA BETA. [250 *k.* 19 (4).] The A B C of musical hand-bell ringing. *Lond.*, 1874, 8vo.
*118. BAKER, W. L. [1743, *e.* 15.] The Great Bell of Westminster, a letter to E. B. Denison, Esq., M.A., Q.C. *Westm.*, 1857, 8vo.
*119. BANISTER, W. [268, *c.* 535.] The Art and Science of Bell-Ringing. [*2nd ed.*] *Lond.*, 1879, 8vo.
120. BATCHELDER, S. Poetry of Bells. *Riverside, U.S.*, 1859, 18mo.
*121. BATTY, REV. R. E. [1743, *e.* 3] Church Bells. [Records of Buckinghamshire . . . together with Transactions of the Architect. and Archæol. Soc. . . . No. 4.] *Aylesbury*, 1855, 8vo.
*122. BEAUFROY, S. [1743, *f.* 1.] The ringer's true guide: containing a safe directory for every true churchman ; or, an affectionate address to ringers in every church and parish. [Inserted after the Preface :—'Memoir of the Rev. S. Beaufroy, of Town Sutton, Kent,' signed S. D. M. ; *n. pl.* (after 1823), 5 leaves.] *Lond.*, 1804, sm. 12mo. ; Ellacombe's Edition, *Lond.*, 1857.
*123. BEAUMONT, W. [1743, *d.* 14.] A chapter on bells and inscriptions upon some of them. *Warrington*, 1888, 8vo.
*124. BENSON, G. [1743, *e.* 19.] The bells of the ancient churches of York. *York*, 1885, 8vo.
*125. BLUNT, W. [46, 1705.] The Use and Abuse of Church Bells with practical suggestions concerning them. *Lond.*, 1846, 8vo.
*126. BRISCOE, J. P. [186, *g.* 202.] Curiosities of the Belfry: with twelve illustrations by Cruikshank, Jewitt and others. *Lond.*, 1883, small 8vo.
*127. BROWN, REV. A. W. [1743, *e.* 5 (1).] The History and Antiquities of Bells and their connection with mythology and ethnology: being part of a paper read (in extract) at the meeting of the Archit. Soc. of the Archdeaconry of Northampton. *Uppingham*, 1857, 8vo.

* Subject Catalogue, Bibl. Bodl., Oxon.

*128. BROWN, REV. A. W. [1743, *e.* 5 (2).] The law of church bells, with suggestions for their legitimate use. Being part of a paper read at Northampton 15th of Oct., 1856, before the Archit. Soc., and of a lecture delivered at Kibworth, 16th Dec., 1856, before the Mutual Improvement Soc. *Lond.* (*Uppingham*), 1857 (*six*), 12mo.

*129. C., LADY H. [250, *k.* 22 (9).] Something about bells told to little folks. *Lond.*, 1878, 8vo.

*130. Campanalogia. [*Mus.* 211, *e.* 5.] Campañalogia improved; or the art of ringing made easy. 5th ed., corrected by J. Monk. *Lond.*, 1866 [1888], 8vo. [*1st ed.*, by F. S., *Lond.*, 1677, 18mo.; *2nd ed.*, 1705; *3rd ed.*, 1733; *4th ed.*, 1753.]

*131. CLARK, J. W. [*G. A., Camb.*, 8vo.] History of the peal of bells belonging to King's Coll., Cambridge. ['Communications . . . Camb. Antiq. Soc.,' vol. iv., p. 223.] *Camb.*, 1881, 8vo.

132. CROOMBE. A Few Words on Bells and Bell-ringing. *Bris.*, 1851, 8vo.

*133. DENISON, E. B. [173, *f.* 11.] Lectures on Church-building; with some practical remarks on bells and clocks [*2nd ed.*]. *Lond.*, 1856, 8vo.

*134. ———— [1743, *e.* 22 (1).] On the Great Bell of Westminster. [(A Paper read before the) Royal Inst. of Great Britain, March 6, 1857.] *n. pl.*, 1857, 8vo.

135. ———— Clocks, Watches and Bells. [*1st ed., Lond.*, 1850, 8vo.; *4th*, 1860; *5th*, 1868; *6th*, 1874; *7th*, 1883.]

136. DIXON. Songs of the Bells. *Lond.*, 1852.

*137. ELLACOMBE, REV. H. T. [173, *e.* 17 (1).] Practical remarks on belfries and ringers. *Lond.*, 1850, 8vo. [*3rd ed., Lond.*, 1871, 8vo. (i. 268, *a.* 53; ii. 268, *a.* 63)].

*138. ———— [*G. Pamp.*, 2448.] Chiming: an appendix to the practical remarks on belfries and ringers. *Lond.*, 1860, 8vo.

*139. ———— [1743, *e.* 17 (2).] Practical remarks on belfries and ringers . . . read with a paper on bells . . . before the Bristol Archit. Soc. . . . Dec. 10, 1849; *2nd ed.*, with an appendix on chiming, with illustrations. *Lond.*, 1861, 8vo.

140. ———— Sermon on the Bells of the Church. *n. pl.*, 1862.

141. ———— History of the Church Bells of Devon, etc. *Exeter*, 1867, 4to.

*142. ———— [*G. A., Devon*, 4to., 10.] The Church Bells of Devon: with a list of those in Cornwall; to which is added a Supplement on various matters relating to the bells of the Church. *Exeter*, 1872, 4to.

143. ELLACOMBE, REV. H. T. The Bells of the Cathedral Church of St. Peter, Exon. *Exeter*, 1874.
*144. —— [*G. A., Somers.*, 4to., 23.] The Church Bells of Somerset; to which is added an Olla Podrida of bell matters of general interest. *Exeter*, 1875, 4to.
*145. —— [*G. A., Gloucs.*, 4to., 21.] The Church Bells of Gloucestershire; to which is added a budget of matters of general interest. *Exeter*, 1881, 4to.
146. EVERARD, G. Bells of St. Peter's, and other papers on Gospel Truth. *Lond.*, 1886, 18mo.
*147. FLETCHER, C. W. [1743, *e.* 20.] Hand-bell ringing. *Lond.*, 1888, 8vo.
*148. FORBES, A. P. [1743, *e.* 2.] Notice of the ancient bell of St. Fillan. [From the Proceedings of the Soc. of Antiqs. of Scot., vol. viii.] *Edinburgh*, 1870 (*eight*), small 4to.
149. FOWLER, J. T. A bell at Pontefract. *York*, 1871, 8vo.
*150. GATTY, A. [47, 933.] The Bell: its origin, history and uses. *Lond.*, 1847, 8vo.; *enlarged*, 1848.
*151. GOSLIN, S. B. [175, *h.* 115 (3).] First steps in bell-ringing. *Lond.*, 1877, 8vo.
*152. —— [174, *e.* 65.] The A B C of musical hand-bell ringing, or the hand-bell ringers' instructor. *Lond.*, 1879, 8vo.
*153. —— [1743, *d.* 18.] *Ibid.*, part 1, 3*rd ed*. *Lond.*, 1887, large 8vo.
*154. —— [1743, *d.* 17.] The musical handbell ringers' instructor, part 2, 2*nd ed*. *Lond.*, 1891, large 8vo.
*155. GOSS, E. H. [1743, *e.* 6.] Early Bells of Massachusetts. (Repr., with additions, from the *Historical and Geneal. Reg.* for April and July, 1874.) *Boston*, 1874 (*fours*), 8vo.
*156. Great Paul. [1743, *e.* 17 (3).] Great Paul tongue-tied, why don't he speak out? By a bell-ringer. *Lond.* (*Hanley*), 1883, small 8vo. [See *post*, 172.]
157. HARRISON, J. Introduction; A Treatise on the Proportion, etc., of Bells. *Hull*, 1835.
*158. HARROD, H. [*G. A., Norf.*, 8vo., 32.] Proceedings relating to the concealment of the sanctus bell at Brampton. [One of the publications of Norfolk and Norwich Archæol. Soc.] *n. pl. or d.* (*c.* 1845), 8vo.
159. HUBBARD. Elements of Campanology. *Ipswich*, 1854; 12mo., 1845.
*160. JOLY, REV. J. S. [170, *f.* 10 (10).] The story of our bell. *Dubl.*, 1881, 8vo.

*161. JONES, W. [268, *b.* 216.] A Key to the Art of Ringing. *Lond., n. d.* (*c.* 1810), 8vo.
*162. —— [*Mus.* 211, *e.* 4.] Clavis Campanalogia, or a Key to the Art of Ringing. *Lond.,* 1888, 8vo.
*163. Journal. *The Bell News and Ringers' Record;* nos. 1, *et seq. Lond.,* 1881-95, 8vo.
*164. —— *Church Bells.* [*n.* 11126, *d.* 7.] *Lond.,* 1871-95.
165. KELSALL, C. Letter on Bells. *Lond.,* 1836, 12mo.
166. L'ESTRANGE, J. Church Bells of Norfolk, with notes on Bells and Bell-founders. *Lond.,* 1874, 8vo.
*167. LLEWELLIN, J., junr. [1743, *e.* 4.] Bells and Bell-founding, a practical treatise upon church bells, by X. Y. Z. [(The dedication signed 'John Llewellin, junior.') With a cutting from *The Engineer,* containing a review of the same.] *Bristol,* 1879, small 4to.
168. LOMAX, B. [174, *g.* 69.] Bells and Bell-ringers. *Lond.,* 1879, 8vo.
*169. LUKIS, W. C. [*G. A., Gen. Top.,* 8vo., 203.] An account of Church bells, with some notices of Wiltshire bells and bellfounders, etc. *Lond.,* 1857, 8vo.
170, 1. —— i. Words to Churchwardens; ii. Ditto to Rural Deans. *Marlboro',* 1858.
*172. MACKAY, J. [*G. A., Lond.,* 8vo., 539.] 'Great Paul,' from its casting to its dedication; with a preface on bells by Sir John Stainer. *Lond.,* 1882, 8vo. [See *supra,* 156.]

[In the course of an interesting and characteristic letter, the genial Oxford Professor of Music recently pointed out 'a very funny misprint' on the frontispiece of this work. 'It is there stated that the Bell is 6 feet 9 inches in diameter, instead of 9 FEET 6 INCHES! It would require a clever founder to get nearly 17 tons of metal into a bell having a diameter of 6 feet 9!']

173. MADGE, SIDNEY J. The History, Traditions, and Peculiar Uses of the Church Bells of Moulton, Northants. *Northampton,* 1893.
174. —— Moulton Church and its Bells; with a Summary of the Bells of Northamptonshire, *Lond.,* 1895, demy 8vo.
175. —— Bells of the City and University of Oxford (with notes, reminiscences, and other communications from the Right Hon. W. E. Gladstone, Lord Salisbury, the Vice-Chancellor, Hon. G. C. Brodrick, Sir John Stainer, and very many others). To be issued shortly. *Lond.*
*176. Management of Bells; a few hints to the clergy, churchwardens, ringers, and others. Being a reprint of a leading article appearing in the *Bell News and Ringers' Record*

of April 15, 1882. [1743, e. 17 (4).] *Lond.*, 1884, small 8vo.
177. MANGAN, C. The Bell: a poem. *n. pl. or d.*
178. MANT, R. The Matin Bell, or the Church Call to Daily Prayer. *Oxf.*, 1848, 12mo.
179. MAUNSELL, W. T. [100, c. 171.] Church bells and ringing. *Lond.*, 1861, 8vo.
180. MONSELL. The Passing Bell: a poem. *Lond.*, 1866.
181. MONTGOMERY, L. I. Dumbarton Bells. *Lond.*, 1884, post 8vo.
182. MOORE. Mysterious ringing of bells at Great Bealings, Suffolk. *Woodbridge*, 1841, 12mo.
183. ——— Church Bells of Walsall. *Walsall*, 1863.
*184. NEWSAM, F. [1743, f. 2.] Our own bells. The substance of an address at one of the 'penny readings' to the children of Hermitage St. Ann's Schools, and others, Hanger Lane, Stamford Hill. By a parishioner. [Preface signed 'F. N.,' Stamford Hill.] *Tottenham*, 1866 (*eights*), 12mo.
*185. NORTH, T. [*G. A., Leics.*, 4to., 8.] The Church Bells of Leicestershire: Their Inscriptions, Traditions, and Peculiar Uses; with chapters on Bells and the Leicester Bellfounders. *Leic.*, 1876, 4to.
*186. ——— [*G. A., Northt.*, 4to., 12.] The Church Bells of Northamptonshire; their inscriptions, traditions, and peculiar uses. *Leic.*, 1878, 4to. [See above, 174.]
*187. ——— [*G. A., Rutl.*, 4to., 3.] The Church Bells of Rutland: their inscriptions, traditions, and peculiar uses; with chapters on bells and bell-founders. *Leic.*, 1880, 4to.
*188. ——— [*G. A., Linc.*, 4to., 11.] The Church Bells of the County and City of Lincoln: their founders, inscriptions, traditions, and peculiar uses; with a brief history of church bells in Lincolnshire, chiefly from original and contemporaneous records. With illustrations. *Leic.*, 1882, 4to.
189. ——— Church Bells of Bedfordshire: their founders, inscriptions, etc. *Lond.*, 1884, 4to.
*190. ——— [*G. A., Herts.*, 4to., 10.] The Church Bells of Hertfordshire: their founders, inscriptions, traditions, and peculiar uses. By the late Tho. North; completed and edited by J. C. L. Stahlschmidt. With illustrations. *Lond.*, 1886 (*fours*), large 8vo.
*191. ——— [1743, d. 12.] English Bells and Bell Lore: a book on bells. Ed. by the Rev. W. Beresford. With illustrations. *Leek*, 1888, 8vo.

192. PAGET, F. E. The Pancake Bell; a poem. *Rugeley*, 1854, 16mo.
193. PEARD, F. M. The Belfry Bell of Bruges. *Lond.*, 1888, 18mo.
*194. PEARSON, C. [1743, *e.* 21.] The Ringers' Guide to the Church Bells of Devon. *Lond. (Exeter)*, 1888, 8vo.
195. POWELL. Touches of Stedman's Triples. *Lond.*, 1828, fol.
*196. RAVEN, J. J. [*G. A., Camb.*, 8vo., 65.] The Church Bells of Cambridgeshire; a chronicle of the principal campanological events that have occurred within the county; to which is appended a list of the inscriptions on the bells. *Lowestoft*, 1869, 8vo.
*197. ——— [1743, *d.* 16.] The Church Bells of Suffolk: a chronicle in nine chapters; with a complete list of the inscriptions on the bells, and historical notes. *Lond.*, 1890, large 8vo.
*198. REEVES, W. [*G. A., Ireland*, 4to., 42 (4).] A historical and descriptive memoir of the Clogan Edachta: commonly known as St. Patrick's bell, or the bell of Armagh. *Dubl.*, 1877, 4to.
*199. RICHARDSON, T. [1743, *e.* 22 (2).] Lessons from the bells. (Sermon on Ps. cxxii. 1.) *n. pl.*, 1892 (*fours*), 8vo.
200. SCHILLER'S Das Lied von der Glocke. Trans. by Anon., 1827; by H. L., 1833; Mangan, 1835; T. B. Lytton, 1839; Montague, 1839; Lambert, 1850; M. Montreal, 1868; Merivale, 1869; and by many others.
*201. SHIPWAY, W. [268, *b.* 120.] The Campanalogia; or, universal instructor in the art of ringing. (In 3 parts.) *Lond.*, 1813-16, 12mo.
*202. SNOWDON, J. W. [268, *c.* 546.] A Treatise on treble bob. (2 parts.) *Leeds*, 1878-79, 8vo.
*203. ——— [268, *c.* 553 (12).] Rope-sight; an Introduction to the Art of Change-ringing. *Leeds*, 1879, 8vo.
*204. ——— [170, *f.* 10 (14, 15).] Standard Methods in the Art of Change-ringing. With diagrams. *Lond.*, 1881, 8vo.
*205. ——— [1743, *e.* 16.] The method of double Norwich Court bob major. *Lond.*, 1884, 8vo.
206. SPURGEON, C. H. Bells for the Horses; a Lecture. *Lond.*, 1869, 18mo.
*207. SOTTANSTALL, W. [174, *g.* 94.] Elements of Campanologia; or an essay on the art of ringing. Part V. *Huddersfield*, 1867, 8vo.
*208. STAHLSCHMIDT, J. C. L. [1743, *e.* 1.] Surrey Bells and

London Bell-founders ; a contribution to the comparative study of bell inscriptions. *Lond.*, 1884, 4to. [See 190.]
209. STEPHENSON, W. F. Changes : Literary, Pictorial, and Musical. *Ripon*, 1857.
210. STEWART, J. S. A Short Touch by a Grandsire Ringer; a poem. *Shifnal*, 1871, 8vo.
211. THACKRAH, B. The art of change-ringing. *Dewsbury*, 1852, 12mo.
*212. THOMPSON, W. H. [1743, *e.* 18.] A note on grandsire triples, showing that the construction of a peal of grandsire triples by means of plain leads and common bob leads only is impossible. *Camb.*, 1886, 8vo.
*213. ———— [1743, *e.* 22 (3).] A diagram of a system of peals of union triples, in imitation of Shipway's peal. *Camb.*, 1893, 8vo.
214. Tintinnalogia ; or the Art of Ringing. *Lond.*, 1668, 12mo.; *Lond.*, 1671 ; also 1700, 'improved by I. White.'
*215. TROYTE, C. A. W. [174, *f.* 3.] Change-ringing: an introduction to the early stages of the art of church or handbell ringing. *Lond.*, 1869, 8vo. ; *2nd ed.*, 1872.
*216. TYSSEN, A. D. [*G. A., Somers.*, 8vo., 42.] The Church Bells of Sussex, with the inscriptions of all the bells in the county. *Lewes*, 1864, 8vo.
*217. VENTRESS, J. [1743, *d.* 1.] The Bells of St. Nicholas' Church, Newcastle-on-Tyne. (From the ' Archæologia Æliana,' vol. ii., new series; 2 drawings.) *Newc.*, 1857 (*six*), large 8vo.
218. WALKER, G. The Midnight Bell. 3 vols. *Lond., n. d.*, 12mo.
219. WIGRAM, W. Change-ringing disentangled. *Lond.*, 1871.
220. ———— Letters on Ringing, a Branch of Church Work. *Camb.*, 1872.
*221. ———— [174, *f.* 52.] Change - ringing disentangled ; with hints on the direction of belfries, on the management of bells, etc. [*2nd ed.*] *Lond.*, 1880, 8vo.
222. WOTY, W. Campanalogia ; a poem in praise of Ringing. *Lond.*, 1761, fol.

SEC. III. MISCELLANEA : 1495 *et seq.*

Comprising Tracts, MSS., and Special Portions of Various Works.

223. BEVERLINCK, L. Conciones selectæ, concio 44, de campanarum usu. *Colon Agrip.*, 1627.
224. BIRINGUCCIO, V. Pirotechnia : cap. x. *Venet.*, 1540,

1550, 1559, 1678 ; Vincent's French Trans., 1556, 1572, 1627.
225. BONA, J.   Rerum liturgicarum, Libri duo: lib. 1, cap. 22. *Romæ*, 1671.
226. BORROMÆUS, C. Liber de Instructione Fabricæ et de Numero campanarum: 'Acta Ecclesiæ Medialanensis.' *Milan*, 1599, 1843, fol.; *Par.*, 1855, fol.
227. BULLETIN MONUMENTAL, tom. xxvi.   Fontenailles Bell.
228. CAMPANI, G. A.   Opera.   *Romæ*, 1495.
229. CASALIUS, J. B.   De profanis et sacris veteribus, ratibus: cap. 43.   *Frankf.*, 1681, 4°.
230. CHATEAUBRIAND, F. A.   Le génerie du chretianisme, vol. iii., c. 1.   *Par.*, 1804.
231. CHRYSANDER, W. C. S. Antiquarische Nachrichten Son Kirchenglocken.   (*Hanöv. Magazin*: vol. v., pt. i., 1754, No. 27.)
232. DICTIONNAIRE des Arts et Metiers: tom. i., pt. 2, p. 709. *Par.*, 1773, 4°.
233. DU FRESNE, C.   Dom. Ducange: Glossario, etc.   *Lugd.*, 1668.
234. DURANDUS, J. S.   De Ritibus Ecclesiæ, lib. 1, c. xxii. *Par.*, 1503, fol.
235. ERSCH AND GRÜBER'S German Cyclopædia.
236. GRILLANDUS, P.   De Sortilegiis ; in Tract. Univ. Juris, vol. xi., pt. 2.
237. HOFMANNUS, J. J.   Lexicon.   *Batavia*, 1694, fol.
238. KIRCHERUS, A.   Musurgia Universalis.   *Romæ*, 1650, fol.
239. LAURENTIUS, J.   Collectio in Jac. Gronovii Thesaur. Græc. Antiqq., tom. viii., col. 1458 ; et Ugolini Thesaur., tom. xxxii., p. 4.
240. LIPENII, M.   Bibliotheca realis Theologica, vol. i.   *Francof.*, 1685.
241. MACER, D.   Hierolexicon.   *Rom.*, 1677, fol.
242. MARTENE, E.   De Antiquis Ecclesiæ Ritibus, lib. iv., c. 2, tom. iii.   *Venet.*, 1783.
243. MENARDUS, H.   Ad librum Sacramentorum Gregorii. *Paris*, 1642, 4°.
244. MERSENNUS.   Harmonicorum, lib. xii.   *Par.*, 1629, 1648.
245. MEYERUS, J. Commentarii seu Annales rerum Flandricarum.   *Antw.*, 1561.
246. MIGNE, J. P. Patrologiæ Cursus Completus, seu Bibliotheca Universalis, etc.   *Par.*, 1844-1864.
247. MUSÆ ANGLICANÆ.   *Oxon.*, 1691.
248. OLEARIUS, J. G.   Additamcuta, etc.   *n. d.*
249. PANCIROLLAS, G.   Nova Repera, Tit. 9.   *Frankf.*, 1603, 4°.

250. PLUCHE, L'ABBÉ. Entretiens xxii., vol. vii. *Par.*, 1762, 12mo.
251. PUFFENDORF, S. Observationibus Jur. Univers., No. 104, p. iv.
252. SALA, R. Rerum Liturg., Card. J. Bonæ, app., tom. ii. *Aug. Taurin*, 1749, 4°.
253. SLEIDANUS, J. Commentar., lib. xxi. *Argent.*, 1555, fol.
254. SUAREZ, F. Defensio Fidei Catholic, lib. ii., c. 16. *Mogunt*, 1630.
255. TELEZ, E. G. Commentar. perpetua Decretalium Gregor., ix., 5 vols. *Macer*, 1756, fol.
256. TRIEST, F. Handbüch zur Berechnung der Baukosten, pt. 12. *Berlin*, 1827.
257. VERGILIUS, P. De Rerum Inventoribus, lib. iii., c. 18. *Neomagi*, 1671.
258. WION, A. Lignum Vitæ. *n. d.*

---

259. ALLEN. Account of Lambeth. *Lond.*, 1826.
260. ANON. A garland of Bells; a poem. *Newc.*, 1815, 12mo.
261. A Poem in praise of Ringing, with plain hints to ringers. *n. pl.*, 1761.
*262. BAGLEY, H. [*Willis MSS., fol.* 43 (26).] A Catalogue of peals of bells, and of bells in and for peals, cast by him. (*Sing. sht.*) *Oxf.*, 1732, fol.
263. BINGHAM, J. Origines Ecclesiasticæ, vols. ii., iii. *Lond.*, 1840.
264. BOWLE. History of Bremhill. *Lond.*, 1828, 8vo.
265. BRAND. Popular Antiquities; Ellis's ed. *Lond.*, 1813, 4to.
266. Calendar, Foster's Perennial. *Lond.*, 1824, 8vo.
267. ———— The Shepherd's. *Lond.*, c. 1644, 18mo.
268. COXE. Christian Ballads. *Oxford*, 1849, 12mo.
269. DAMAN, MISS. Church Bells; a poem. *Lond.*, 1864.
270. Encyclopædia, Edinburgh: Horology, by Rev. M. S. Ludham. *Edinb.*, 1830.
271. ———— Penny: Bell, by Sir Henry Ellis. *Lond.*, 1835.
272. ———— Various, *ad libitum*.
273. HONE. Every Day and Year Book. *Lond.*, 1827-35.
274. LAMBERT. Country-man's Treasure, etc. *Lond. Br., n. d.*, 12mo.
*275. LESTER, T. [*Willis MSS., fol.* 43 (27).] List of Bells cast by Thomas Lester, from Aug. 1738; single sheet. *n. pl. or d.*, fol.
276. Manual, Brassfounder's. *Lond.*, 1829.
*277. MENEELY, E. A. [1743, *d.* 10.] [Catalogue of] E. A. and

G. R. Meneely, bell-founders, West Troy, N.Y. *West Troy*, 1870, large 8°.
278. Midland Counties Historical Collection, 3 vols. *Leic.*, 1854-56, 8vo.
279. MSS.—Corbet, Bp. [*Ashm. MSS.* 36, 37, *fol.* 260, 261.] To Younge Tom of Christ Church.
280. —————— Laughton, W. Remarks and Performances of a Rambling Club of Ringers; their famous exploits in the art of Ringing. *Guildhall Lib., Lond.*
281. —————— Osborn. [*Add. MSS., Nos.* 19, 368 *and* 19,373, *Brit. Mus.*]
282. —————— Orders of the Company of Ringers in Cheapside, 1603. [*MS. cxix., All Souls' Lib., Oxf.*]
283. —————— Proprietates Campanarum. [*Rawl. MSS. B.* 332, *memb. soc. xv. Bodleian.*]
284. —————— Orders of the Company of the Western Green Caps, 1683. [*Ibid.*, Misc. 834.]
285. —————— The ringing of bells in changes or varying of numbers. [*Ibid.*, A. 315 and f. 215 *b*, sec. xvij.]
286. —————— Palmer, H. Verses on Ringing and Changes, in Hebrew, Greek, Latin, and English, 1658. [*Ibid.*, Misc. MSS. 1,144.] *Bodleian Lib., Oxford.*
287. Nature displayed, vol. vii. *Lond.*, 1763, 12mo.
*288. RUDDALL, ABR. [*Fol. O.* 662 (44).] A catalogue of peals of bells, and of bells in and for peals; cast since the year of our Lord 1684. *Oxf.*, 1715, fol.; another, *Glouc.*, 1751, fol.: Willis MSS., fol. xliii. (25); a third, *Glouc.*, *n. d.*, fol.; Scrap Book I.
289. RAMSAY, DEAN. Letter to the Lord Provost of Edinburgh, on the expediency of providing the city with an efficient peal of bells. *Edinb.*, 1859.
290. The School of Recreation; or, Gentleman's Tutor in various Exercises. *n. pl.*, 1684.
291. SCHOLESFIELD. Supplement to 'The Clavis.' *Huddersfield*, 1853.
292. STAVELEY. History of Churches. *Lond.*, 1773, 8vo.
293. TANSUR. Elements of Music, c. x. *Lond.*, 1772, 8vo.
294. THEOPHILUS (c. 1200 A.D.). Treatises, 3 vols.; transl. by Hendrie. *Lond.*, 1847, 8vo.
295. TRACTS.—Matin Bells and the Curfew. *Oxon.*, 1852.
296. —————— Miller. Church Bells. *Lond.*, 1843, 12mo.
297. —————— Plain Hints to Bell-ringers; Par. Tr., 47. *Lond.*, 1852.
298. —————— Scudamore Chimes. *Lond.*, 1871, 18mo.
299. —————— Suggestions on the Devotional use of the Curfew. *n. pl.*, 1860.

300. TRACTS.—The Passing Bell. *Lond., n. d.*
301. ———— Walsh. Midnight Bells: a poem. *n. pl. or d.*
302. ———— Wolfe. Address on the science of campanology. *Lond.*, 1851.
303. ———— Wolsey's Bell in Sherborne Abbey Church, with a Sermon by the Bishop of Oxford. *Sherborne*, 1866.
*304. WARNER, J., AND SONS. [1743, *d*. 13.] Bell Catalogue. *Lond.*, 1877, large 8vo.

PERIODICAL LITERATURE: 1730-1895.

SEC. IV. SIGNED ARTICLES, ETC.

305. A.D. 1684. Husbandman's Mag.: The Noble Recreation of Ringing, by T. S.
306. A.D. 1754. Hanöv. Magazin., vol. v., pt. 1, No. 27.
307. 1843. Vorhandlung des Vereins des Gewerbfleisses. Sept., Oct.
308. 1856-57. Penny Post: numerous articles.
309. 1861. Parish Magazine: Our Bells and their Ringers.
310. DENISON, E. B. On Casting and Ringing of Large Bells: Proceedings of Inst. Brit. Archits., 1856.
311. DICKENS, C. Ancient College Youths: All the Year Round, 1869.
312. DOHERTY, J. J. Church Bells in England: Month, Nov., 1890.
313. ELLACOMBE, Rev. H. T. Illus. paper on Bells: Rep. Bristol Archit. Soc., 1850.
314. FEASEY, H. J. Gossip on Church Bells: Newb. House M., Aug., 1893.
315. FOWLER, Rev. J. T. Campanology: Union Review; also Gent. M., iii., vol. xix., 1865: note on p. 402.
316. GORDON, W. J. Bell Mottoes: Sund. Home, April, 1890.
317. GOSS, E. H. Bells: New Eng. M., Jan., 1891.
318. GUTHRIE, E. Glasgow for Bells: Leis. Hr., July, 1893.
319. HADDON, J. C. Inscriptions on Bells: Newb. House M., Oct., 1891.
320. HAWEIS, Rev. H. R. Bells and Carillons: Contemp. Rev., 1870-71.
321. ———— Bells and Belfries: Eng. Illus., Feb., 1890.
322. HURELL, E. M. The Italian Campaniles: New Eng. M., Nov., 1893.
323. MACCARTHY, D. F. The Legend of the Limerick Bellfounder: Dubl. Univ. M., 1847.
324. MADGE, S. J. Moulton Bells: Northampton Herald, Nov. and Dec., 1893.

325. MADGE, S. J. Oxford and Oxfordshire Bells, Bell-founders, and Belfries: a Christmas contribution to the 'Oxford Times,' 1894. Six columns. *Reprinted*, Jan. 1895.
326. ——— References to Northamptonshire Bells in Founders' Catalogues: 'Northants Notes and Queries,' vol. vi., pt. xliii., July, 1894.
327. ——— 'Great Paul's' Journey through Northamptonshire, MDCCCLXXXII.; with ordnance heights and other topographical features: Northampton Herald, April 13th, 1895; *reprinted* (20 copies) April 17th. Also 'N. N. and Q.,' pt. xliv., Oct., 1894.
328. ——— Records of Moulton Bells: 'N. N. and Q.,' pt. xlv., Jan., 1895.
329. PALEY, W. B. Bells and their Makers: Gent. M., March, 1893.
330. PEACOCK, F. Some Lincolnshire Bell Customs: Reliq., July, 1893.
331. WOODFORD, W. F. Bell Lore: Ring's Own, Oct., 1893.

SEC. V. GENERAL MATTERS ABOUT BELLS, ETC.

Antiq., vol. 4; Appleton's J.,* 11; Argosy, vol. 18, and for years 1844, '48, '52, '65; Belgra., 28; Bent. Misc., 9; Builder, 1874; Cath. World, 2; Cham. Edinb. J., 24, 28, 42, 47, 64; Ecclesiolog., 1856-7; Gent. M., 57, 82, 83, 99, 100; n.s. 35; Good Words, 20; Harper's M., 40; Leis. Hour, 5, 9; Month, 35, 54; Month. Relig. M., 67; Music. Gazette, 1856-7; Notes and Queries, series i. 3; ii. 5; Once a Week, 3; Penny M., 3; Quar. R., 95.

BELFRIES.—Amer. Architect, 13; Archæolog., 37; Art J., 25; Gent. M., series i. 96; iii. 7. Blackened: Notes and Queries, iv. 9; detached: N. Q., i. 7-9; ii. 3; vii. 9, 10; etymology: N. Q., vi. 5, 6, 12; inscriptions: N. Q., vi. 1; rhymes: N. Q., ii. 11, iii. 6; rules: N. Q., v. 5; vi. 1; Saxon bell-house: N. Q., i. 4; song: N. Q., vi. 1.

FOUNDERS.—Acad., 26; Gent. M., i. 8, 9; iii. 9, 16; N. Q., iii. 6; v. 5, 9; vi. 2-4, 6, 8; vii. 6, 9, 12; Reliq., 13. Ancient: N. Q., iii. 5, 8, 9; bells and clocks: Penn. M., 11; Braziers: N. Q., iii. 10; in 1722: ii. 2; John de Stafforde: iii. 9; Marc le Ser: viii. 12; temp. Edw. VI.: v. 3; Rudhalls: vii. 12.

INSCRIPTIONS.—Gent. M., series i., vols. 58, 60, 99 (pt. 2); ii. 29; iii. 16. N. Q., i. 6, 8-12; ii. 1-5, 7, 8, 10-12; iii. 1, 3, 4, 7-11; iv. 3-7, 9-12; v. 1-6, 8-12; vi. 1, 5, 6, 8, 9; vii. 1-4, 6, 9, 10, 12. Sat. R., vol. 60.

* J., Journal; M., Magazine; R., Review. All references, unless stated otherwise, are to the *volumes*: it is unnecessary to refer here to the pages, as the several indexes will supply these.

RINGERS AND RINGING.—Antiq. (n.s.), 3 ; Chamb. Ed. J., 54, 55 ; Ev. Sat., 9 ; Gent. M., i. 73, 91, 98, 99 (pt. 2) ; ii. 12 ; Leis. Hr., 26 ; N. Q., i. 10, 12 ; ii. 1 ; iii. 12 ; iv. 2, 4, 7, 12. 'Auker' : N. Q., ii. 8 ; vii. 10 ; contests : vii. 11, 12 ; customs : vii. 9 ; electricity : Gent. M., i. 80 ; epitaphs : N. Q., iv. 1 ; vi. 5 ; fines : iii. 7 ; Italian : ii. 6, 7 ; Northern and Sherwood Youths : ii. 8 ; rules : iv. 3 ; societies : iii. 11 ; terms used : i. 5 ; vi. 2 ; tablets : iv. 3 ; women ringers : v. 5.

SEC. VI. SPECIAL MATTERS ABOUT BELLS.

Advent : N. Q., i. 1 ; vii. 6, 7 ; after service : i. 9, 10 ; agreement : ii. 12 ; alphabet : iv. 1 ; vi. 4 ; ancient : Amer. Archtct., 23 ; Antiq. (n.s.), 3 ; New Eng. Hist. Reg., 28, 37 ; N. Q., i. 10 ; iv. 9, 11 ; vi. 6 ; angelus : iv. 1, 11 ; vi. 5 ; animalculæ : Gent. M., i. 58 ; Pop. Sci. R., 1 ; archæology : Antiq., 2, 3 ; N. Q., ii. 9.

Baptism : N. Q., i. 7 ; iii. 4 ; iv. 10 ; v. 3 ; Big Ben and others : Leis. Hr., 26 ; blessing : Congreglst., 6.

Cage : N. Q., iii. 10 ; chimes : J. Frankln. Inst., 113, 114 ; Leis. Hr., 9, 26 ; N. Q., vi. 5 ; Potter's Amer. Month., 11 ; Christmas : N. Q., vi. 10 ; clocks : v. 9, 10 ; cloth b. : v. 6, 7 ; coins : v. 2, 4, 5 ; coomb : vi. 5 ; cracked : Gent. M., 1864 ; N. Q., iii. 1 ; curfew : Gent. M., 93, 94 ; N. Q. iv. 2, 6 ; vi. 5-8.

Death : N. Q., i. 2, 7-9, 12 ; v. 1 ; vi. 2 ; viii. 5, 6 ; dedication : Antiq., 13 ; N. Q., vi. 5 ; destroyed : iii. 9 ; dissenters' rights, etc. : i. 2, 4 ; iv. 4 ; dumb : Gent. M., 16.

Easter : N. Q., i. 11 ; etymology : vi. 7.

Fire : N. Q., ii. 6 ; flax b. : vii. 2, 3.

Glass : N. Q., ii. 8. ; gleaning : vi. 12 ; vii. 4 ; greatest ringing b. : J. Frankln. Inst., 114.

Hermit's b. : N. Q., vi. 11, 12 ; Hieronymus Magius : Sat. Rev., 59 ; history : Gent. M., i. 8, 34, and for 1855 ; J. Frankln. Inst., 5 : Month : 64 ; South. R. (n.s.), 22.

Legends : Blackwd., 83 ; Gent. M. 1864 ; N. Q., ii. 7 ; iv. 5, 8 ; Sharpe's Lond. M., 30 ; lists of peals : Gent. M., 82, 88 ; N. Q., i. 1, 4 ; iii. 4 ; iv. 3, 4 ; literature : i. 9-11 ; ii. 5 ; iii. 4, 6, 12 ; iv. 1, 2, 5, 8 ; v. 3-5, 9 ; vii. 5, 6.

Metal : All Yr. Round, 24 ; Ev. Sat., 9 ; N. Q., ii. 8 ; iii. 2 ; iv. 1 ; v. 4 ; viii. 3 ; Pract. M., 3 ; morning b. : N. Q., vi. 6 ; vii. 3, 9.

North's Works on Church Bells : Athenæum, 1887.

Pagan : N. Q., vii. 8 ; pancake : v. 11 ; pardon : i. 11 ; passing : i. 5, 8 ; iii. 2, 5, 12 ; iv. 7, 8 ; v. 11, 12 ; vii. 5 ; viii. 3, 4 ; Poe's poem : New Eng. Hist. Reg. 3 ; priests' b. : N. Q., v. 4, 5 ; vii. 5 ; private chapel b. : v. 11.

Rhymes : N. Q., iv. 4 ; v. 2, 3 ; vi. 9 ; Roman : vii. 3 ; royal heads on b. : iv. 9, 12 ; v. 1, 2, 4, 5, 9.

Bibliotheca Campanalogica 97

Saints' b. : N. Q., vi. 2, 3; sanctus and sacring: i. 10, 11; iv. 1, 8, 9; vi. 6; vii. 10; sanctus cotes: iv. 9; vi. 4-7; sermon b. : i. 11; v. 3, 4; silver: ii. 1; v. 9; skelets: iii. 5; song: v. 12; vi. 1; spirits: Leis. Hr., 23; stamp: N. Q., vi. 2; steel: i. 12; ii. 1; storm: vi. 2, 3; submerged: i. 10, 11; ii. 10; subterranean: i. 7.

Tocsin : N. Q., iv. 8; voices: Chamb. Ed. J., 19; N. Q., vii. 12, viii. 3; wooden b. : ii. 1, 5.

SEC. VII. TOPOGRAPHICAL REFERENCES.

ABERDEEN : N. Q., vi. 2, 3. Aberdovey : iii. 6. America: iii. 12; vii. 4. Ashover (Derbys.): iii. 9. Avignon: Cath. World, 1. Ayston (Rutl.): v. 10, 11. Ballarat : iv. 3. Batley: iii. 9. Bedfordshire : Antiq. (n.s.), 9. Belfast (St. Patrick's Bell): Gent. M., ii. 35. Berwick: N. Q., i. 8. Bewdley : iv. 8. Bex, Canton de Vaux : iv. 10. Birmingham : v. 4. Blakesley: vi. 2. Bletchley : i. 12. Bolton-by-Bowlands (Yorks.) : iv. 9. Bordeaux: iii. 3. Botreaux : Blackwd., 83. Brailes (Warwicks.) : N. Q., iv. 5; v. 9. Bray: v. 3. Brigstock : iv. 1. Brinney: iv. 3. Brinsop (Heref.) : iv. 12.

Cambridgeshire : Gent. M., iii. 18; N. Q., iv. 12; vi. 2, 3; Sat. Rev., 54. Cardonagh: Gent. M., i. 98. Carlisle : Nationl. R. 5. Cheltenham: N. Q., iv. 9. Cheshire : Gent. M., iii. 17; N. Q., vii. 1. China: ii. 8. Church-Kirk (Blackburn): iv. 9. Clapton-in-Gordano (Somers.): iv. 6. Cold Ashby (Northants): iv. 11. Cork : iv. 6. Cornwall : N. Q., iii. 8; Reliq. 14-18. Coventry: N. Q., iii. 9; iv. 6, 7. Cubberley (Glouc.), iv. 10. Culmington : iii. 6.

Derbyshire : Reliq., 13-18. Dublin: N. Q., iv. 2, 3. Dunmer : vi. 1. Durham : vii. 12.

East Anglia : Gent. M., iii. 10. Edinburgh : Gent. M., 15. Essex : Antiq. (n.s.), 18; N. Q., ii. 7

Fiji Islands ; N. Q., ii. 9. Frinsbury (Kent): iv. 6. Glasgow : Gent. M., 60. Gloucestershire: N. Q., vi. 5. Haddenham : N. Q., v. 2. Hants : v. 6. Harbledown : iv. 3. Hastings : iii. 6. Hedon: i. 12. Holbeck Lunds Chapel (Yorks.) : iv. 12. Holmes Chapel (Cheshire) : v. 5. Holywood (Dumfries): iv. 8. Hordley: v. 12.

Ireland : Gent. M., ii. 37; N. Q., vii. 12; viii. 4. Italy: ii. 7. Ivinghoe : v. 5.

Kensington : Gent. M., i. 91; N. Q., iv. 3. Kent: Antiq. (n.s.), 17; Sat. R., 65. Kirkthorpe : N. Q., iii. 11, 12.

Lande-Fleurie : Overl. Monthly (n.s.), 18. Lansallos: N. Q., i. 11. Leicestershire: v. 6. Leighton (Hunts): v. 6. Lichfield : v. 12. Limerick : Archæologia, 37; Dubl. Univ. M., 30;

N. Q., i. 1, 2, 6; iv. 3; v. 3. Lincolnshire: Gent. M., i. 37, 78, 99 (pt. 2), 101; N. Q., v. 12; vi. 2, 3. London: Chamb. Edinb. J., 67; Gent. M., i. 58, 92 (pt. 2); ii. 6; N. Q., iii. 5; v. 1, 7, 9; (St. Paul's): Longman's, 13-15; N. Q., iv. 5, 7; Sat. R., 53.

Malta: N. Q., iii. 2. Margate: i. 1. Massachusetts, U.S.A.: New Eng. Hist. Reg., 28. Moscow (Russia): Gent. M., ii. 6; N. Q., ii. 8; iv. 1, 3, 7.

Norfolk: N. Q., iii. 10; iv. 5. Northampton.: v. 5. Northfield (Worcs.) iv. 9. North-Otterington: v. 1. Norton: v. 6. Norwich: ii. 7. Nottinghamshire: Reliq., 13.

Ornoloe: N. Q., iii. 11. Osney (near Oxford): Gent. M., 101; N. Q., ii. 1; iii. 2. Oxford: ii. 2, 10; iii. 2, 8; iv. 5, 9; vi. 5.

Paisley: N. Q., v. 8. Passenham (Norf.): iv. 9. Peterborough: iii. 2, 9. Philadelphia (U.S.A.): ii. 4. Pisa (Italy): iii. 2, 3. Plymouth: iii. 6. Puncknowle: iii. 8.

Quendon: Gent. M., 76. Quimper (Normandy): N. Q., viii. 3.

Rhos Crowther: N. Q., vi. 9. Rome: Gent. M., iii. 7; N. Q., iv. 7. Romford: i. 11. Rouen (France): i. 9. Rowleston (Heref.): iv. 10.

Sans Blas: Atlant. Month., 50. Sans Gabriel: Lippinc. M., 48. Santa Theresa Convent: N. Q., i. 7. Scotland: Gent. M., ii. 37. Seckington (Warwicks.): N. Q., v. 8. Sheffield: vi. 8. Shipton-le-Moyne: iii. 10. Shrewsbury: Gent. M., 100; N. Q., iv. 3. Shropshire: vii. 12. Southfleet (Kent): iv. 12. Spain: Gent. M., ii. 6; N. Q., iii. 4. St. Andrew's (Fife): iii. 11; vii. 12. St. Ceneu: iii. 6; v. 4. St. Keyne's (Cornwall): ii. 11. Stafford: Athenæum, 1889. Stepney: N. Q., iv. 7. Surrey: Acad., 26; N. Q., iii. 6; v. 6.

Tadley (Hants): N. Q., vi. 9. Tanfield: iii. 6. Tetney (Lincs.): vi. 3. Tottenham: iv. 2; v. 5. Tresmeer (Cornwall): vi. 8, 9. Trim: Gent. M., ii. 41.

Ware: N. Q., viii. 3. Warwickshire: iii. 10; v. 3. Waterford: iv. 9. Wednesbury: v. 3, 4. Wells: ii. 4. Westminster: Archæologia, 37; Gent. M., 96; Leis. Hr., 24; N. Q., iii. 7; iv. 6, 8. Weston: iii. 10. Whitechapel: viii. 2, 3. Wigan: vii. 12; viii. 2. Wimbledon: iii. 6. Worcester: iii. 8, 9; iv. 3, 9; vi. 3.

Yarnscombe (Devon): N. Q., v. 9, 10. Yarrick: Chamb. Edinb. J., 57. Yorkshire: Gent. M., ii. 44; N. Q. iii. 12; vi. 2; vii. 7.

Non vox sed votum non musica cordula sed cor.

THE END.

Elliot Stock, 62, Paternoster Row, London.

www.ingramcontent.com/pod-product-compliance
Lightning Source LLC
Chambersburg PA
CBHW031119160426
43192CB00008B/1050